THE POWER OF BEING A _REAL_ WOMAN!

A compilation of the most empowering, educating, equipping, encouraging, practical and motivating ways to become the woman you've always wanted to be!

JENNIFER KEITT

Host/Founder
Today's Black Woman Radio Show Inc.

Today's Black Woman Corporation Publishing

The Power Of Being A Real Woman!
© 2001 by Jennifer Keitt,
Today's Black Woman Corporation.
All rights reserved.

Published by TODAY'S BLACK WOMAN
CORPORATION PUBLISHING
888-TB-WOMAN

Visit our website at www.todaysblackwomanradio.com

First Edition

ISBN: 0-9711141-0-2

To the most important people in my life:
my Lord Jesus Christ,
my husband, Tony,
and my children,
Morgan,
Naomi,
Caleb
and Samantha...
I finally did it!

CONTENTS

Introduction

INTRODUCTION

Let The Journey Begin!

Ladies, are you ready to take your life to the next level? Then I dare you to strip off your mask, let go of what *"they say,"* what *"they think"* and what your own mind is saying and come on a journey with me. This journey will lead you toward the place of becoming the woman you've always wanted to be!

I've compiled this book based on over ten years of probing, searching and learning about the never-ending, fascinating state of being a woman. Through my radio show, web site and numerous speaking engagements around the country, I've heard women and I've seen the weights, baggage, frustration and pain that we carry. So I decided to write this book for you; to bless you, to encourage you and to motivate you toward that place you've always wanted to be in your life!

I'd like to start our time together with one simple declaration: There's POWER in being a REAL woman!

You might think the concept of being "real" strange, but it isn't. You see, far too many women don't know how to be real. We've constructed fake shells that we "put on" for our families, our significant others, our friends and the world, while on the inside we really don't support, appreciate or even like ourselves. Many women don't trust our own decision-making abilities. We've learned to hide our true feelings to the point of walking around void of the essence of who we really are, what we really want and where we really want to go in life: we're no longer "in touch" with our true selves. We live life every day never "feeling real," and are building our lives on no firm foundation within. With our authenticity gone, we tend to feel false and our hearts have turned to hardened shells. The bottomline is that life has become a never-ending cycle in which we hide our true selves and our true feelings to please others. Not in a normal, healthy, helping and sacrificing way, but in the costly pouring out of our damaged souls without having substance and real power on the inside. Burying our vibrancy, our brilliancy, our glow and shine...we've lost the real woman within.

Well, I say, not any more—it's time for change!

Change is the process of letting go of who we are to become the women we want to be! Remember, we will grow and change only to the degree that we willingly participate in our own process of change.

YOU, and only you, MUST CHOOSE TO CHANGE!

Ladies, have courage! Don't be afraid. Let's begin to get an understanding that our lives are a series of movements and seasons that catapult us from one level of glory to the next! With this movement, hopefully, we are moving closer and closer to our destinies and purposes, closer to the Lord, and closer to lives full of abundance and excitement.

So, what is change? And how can we use change to get to our next level?

Change, by definition is, "transformation, to make radically different, or undergoing transformation."

"...but be transformed (changed) by the (entire) renewal of your mind (by its new ideals and its new attitude) so that you may prove (for yourselves) what is the good and acceptable and perfect will of God..." Romans 12:2 (amplified)

Transformation in our life will happen when we get a new "mind-set," a "new attitude," and a fresh God-perspective on life! We want new things, new lives? Then we've got to change our old ways of thinking, believing and acting. The only tried and proven way of changing my thinking has been through the Word of God, His Bible—taking in, reading, meditating and studying the Word to get God's thoughts, hopes and plans for me in my heart and mind.

We've tried the affirmations and the positive thinking, but we are still stuck. Today's woman is ready for true, long-lasting change. When true transformation takes place, as women we move into position to prove for ourselves the perfect will of God in our lives! Our esteem rises, our marriages change, our families change, our lives become full, complete and prosperous and we move into the position of living abundant lives!

This is the most exciting place to be for today's woman! To no longer be subject to everyone else and their plan for us, but to become free to live a life that is pleasing to us and to our God!

The 3 stages of change are:

1.   Becoming aware. Change begins to take place when we become aware of our thinking, feelings and

behaviors. During this self-discovery, we must become aware of the wounds in our lives and then open up to God's restoration process. We can't remain in denial. Denial is a form of bondage. We must become aware of our feelings, actions and thoughts that come from our woundedness so that we can cooperate with the Lord's restoration work in our lives.

2.   *Becoming responsible.* We then become responsible for ourselves and for the state that our lives are in right now. This includes responsibility for our feelings, our thoughts and our behaviors AND for our response to how others treat us. Don't ever become a victim of being a victim—That place of thinking and responding to life situations as a victim all the time. Once we become aware, then we move on to accepting the responsibility for where we are in life; we can then become responsible for ourselves, no longer blaming the past or others so that we can change and grow

3.   *Becoming FREE.* *"And you shall know the truth and the truth shall make you free," John 8:32.* Freedom is that place of knowing God, loving and living our lives free from the demands, situations and circumstances of life and other people! Freedom is automatic when we become women aware of who we are and how we feel, then we move into taking and accepting responsibility for our life and the state we are in, then we move into being open to the "truth" of God's healing and restoration—and to the degree that we know truth, the truth that we know WILL MAKE US FREE! This is awesome news!

It's time to begin, let's make a decision to change with the goal of moving our lives forward! I will accept no less than total and complete change in the major areas of my life; I encourage you to do the same. Make a decision right now to make a move:

1. Relationally (in our key relationships)
2. Emotionally (in our mind, will and feelings)
3. Spiritually (in the inner woman of our hearts)

Let's begin with a quick general life assessment of where we are at this current moment (sort of establishing the BEFORE picture!) This is crucial in moving into the place of taking off our masks and becoming REAL women. Be honest about where you are in the following areas of your life.

Evaluate Your Life!
Please check all responses that apply.

- **SPIRIT**
  _____Dead (I don't know where God and I stand with one another)
  _____Alive (I'm in a love relationship with God, through His Son, Jesus Christ, and it's getting better daily!)
- **SOUL**
  _____Emotionally strong and thriving
  _____Emotionally weak, suffering
  _____Confident, normal self-esteem
  _____Low, non-confident self-esteem
- **BODY**
  _____Actively taking care of body
  _____Not taking care of body
  _____Happy with current weight/size
  _____Not happy with current weight/size

- **RELATIONSHIPS**—Significant social relationships (include dating relationships if not married)

  _____Relationship(s) overall okay, continuing to work on making them better

  _____Relationship(s) overall not okay, ceased trying to make them better or don't know how to make them better

- **FINANCES**

  _____Current financial affairs are stable and getting better

  _____Current financial affairs are a mess, worse and declining

- **EMOTIONAL/PHYSICAL HEALTH**

  _____Emotional health stable and getting better

  _____Emotional health bad and getting worse

  _____Physical health is great (free of stress, worry, anxiety)

  _____Physical health is all right (battling with stress, worry, anxiety occasionally)

  _____Physical health is not good at all; I am suffering

- **WOMAN—MYSELF**

  _____I am happy and content with myself and where I am right now in my life in general

  _____I am NOT happy and content with myself and where I am right now in my life

- **WIFE—HUSBANDS**

  _____My marriage is right "on-the-money"—great and getting better daily (with normal challenges daily)

  _____My marriage is horrible, I am not happy with my mate and I don't see any chance of it getting better

- **MOTHER—CHILDREN**
  _____My individual relationship(s) with my child(ren) is normal, happy and healthy, improving and growing daily

  _____My relationships with my children are not good.

How do you feel about your overall life? Based on the mini-assessment, are there areas for change? You know that I know that there are areas you want to change so let's get started! Below are ten simple keys to help make change easier.

Ten Keys Women Need To Know About Change In Our Lives

1. **NO MORE TRYING TO CHANGE.** We must *allow* change to happen.
2. **WE MUST FIND A WAY TO UNDERSTAND THE NEED FOR CHANGE IN OUR LIVES.** Asking, seeking and knocking all of the time until we find the answers that we need inside God, inside ourselves, inside others…so we can be comfortable with wherever we are in our lives.
3. **WITH UNDERSTANDING WE CAN BEGIN SEEING CLEARER.** We can celebrate having new vision to see change is possible. We must engage in a change of focus. We may need to regroup, wipe tears, dry our nose, scrap off our knees, wipe the dirt off our hands and faces and reset our vision to see the impossible, to see right through to change on the other side.
4. **HOPE NEEDS TO BE REKINDLED INSIDE US.** We must have the blueprint to get to change, and hope is that blueprint. It shows us what we desire and keeps our vision focused until we have

completed the transformation to get to the change to get us to our desired destination...where our purpose and destiny and ultimate happiness and fulfillment lies!

5. **WE SHOULD BECOME GOAL-ORIENTED.** We must know that we will be better than we are right now—we must set realistic goals for change, one area at a time, and pursue them until change is a reality in every area of our lives.

6. **START RIGHT NOW, RIGHT HERE** Change is now--right now--not tomorrow, not yesterday--right now! What stage are we in?

7. **RECOGNIZE OUR NEED FOR HELP.** Realize we must not and can not be an island unto ourselves. Help is always going to be needed, especially the help of our Heavenly Father!

8. **GET REACQUAINTED WITH BELIEF IN OURSELVES.** We *know* we can change. If not another soul believes in us, or that change is possible even for us, *we must believe in ourselves and know that change is available!*

9. **RECOGNIZE OUR PAST MISTAKES, BUT DON'T DWELL THERE.** Leave our past behind! Leave our regrets, should-ofs, could-ofs, would-ofs, leave blame and offense behind. *...but one thing I do—it is my one aspiration—forgetting what lies behind and straining forward to what lies ahead, I press on... Philippians 3:13*

10. **NOTHING CAN STOP US NOW EXCEPT OURSELVES.** Be forewarned that the only enemy to change in our lives is ourselves! Don't be caught sleeping with the enemy and it's you!

Personal Thoughts:

CHAPTER ONE

A *Real* Woman—
The Power Of Being Real

"...For her worth is far above rubies."
Proverbs 31:10

There's power in being REAL! Real means *not artificial or fraudulent;* it means *genuine; being precisely what the name implies.* We can't discuss being real without talking about its partner, transparency. To be transparent means *to be free from pretense or deceit; frank; easily seen through; obvious; readily understood; clear.*

When we are not phony or deceptive but we become transparent and live our lives based on "what you see is what you get," then life begins to take on a whole new meaning! The ability to become transparent with ourself first and then with others is a major life-principle that will change our world and create the kind of life that is worth living!

Finding and Knowing the Real me...
"...She perceives that her merchandise is good"
Proverbs 31:18

Think about this. Every day of our lives we enter into our world and we exchange ourselves, the *merchandise of our souls*—love, joy, ideas, thoughts, feelings, our hopes, dreams and desires with our spouses, our families, our colleagues, co-workers and friends.

If we were to begin to get *real*, many of us would admit that we don't feel that we have very good inner merchandise. Many would say we don't feel that our goods and commodities are worthy of sale or exchange in anyone else's life. For far too many of us the *real* woman inside is bruised, broken, tattered, frustrated, discouraged and barely surviving. Our inner merchandise is damaged, squelched, suppressed and in many cases extinguished…just plain gone.

Well, today, help is on the way!

Step One: Finding
"She girds her arms with strength and strengthens her arms."
Proverbs 31:17

Too often we get caught up in *doing* and *existing* and forget all about living life! We forget that we are the ones in charge of our lives—not our bosses, boyfriends, children and everyone else.

A real woman recognizes that it is her job to "gird her arms with strength and strengthen her arms." This means that we should be in a constant state of preparedness. We should be continually preparing ourselves spiritually, mentally and physically for our lives.

This preparation can't and won't happen if we refuse the important task of finding and knowing ourselves, knowing our desires, executing our plans, fulfilling our purposes and walking the road toward our destinies. Finding and knowing ourself starts with being truthful in your heart and then it takes the determination and commitment of taking care of ourself, our complete self: spirit, soul and body.

So with this in mind, let's start with cleaning house by doing a clean sweep of our inner selves.

Clean Sweep
"Casting ALL your care upon Him, for He cares for you."
1 Peter 5:7

To cast means *to throw, to fling, to toss.* A care is *a distraction.* A clean-sweep is *to throw, fling and toss our distractions and cares.* Cares divide us. Cares cause us to be disunited. Cares part us from our peace, from our joy, from our happiness, from our families, friends and from our lives. A house divided won't stand and neither will a woman who is divided by inner turmoil through cares and circumstances of life. Cares choke your life. When we play with forty items over and over in our minds, performing mental gymnastics with problems, goals, issues or cares, we begin to lose focus, and lose sight of the real woman within who is waiting to burst free into a life that she can love. When our cares begin to choke us and begin to squeeze the quality of life from within us, we slowly but surely begin to become one with our cares. Becoming one with our cares is like being taken by the throat, cutting off our air supply and having our life slowly sucked out of us. The real us ceases to have power and we begin to become a bundle of nerves and cares. Out of our heart spills cares, concerns and worries, discontentment, anxiety and fear. Our thoughts are consumed by cares and this is a key indicator the real us is gone and we've become one with our cares!

Selah...Pause, Think and TAKE ACTION
Break FREE from your cares—make a clean sweep

We are going to begin the process of eliminating what is draining us and weighting us down! We're not going to leave our goal of becoming real women. We are going to use this exercise to take an honest, transparent look behind the scenes in our minds.

Below please list the top ten thoughts that are weighing on your mind right now. What cares, thoughts or concerns occupy your head right now? What's on your mind? Don't give this deep thought; simply begin writing the items as they pop into your head. Don't leave out anything. Keep writing until the initial flow stops (list everything from bills to manicures and from hurt feelings to job issues). The amount here doesn't matter, just get it out. If it's less that ten things—great. But if you need more paper that's fine too! (smile)

1. _____

2. _____

3. _____

4. _____

5. _____

6. _____

7. _____

8. _____

9. _____

10. _____

Now, take a deep breath. Listen. There shouldn't be any more "noise" left in your head; it's all sitting right here in front of you on paper. It's out! Doesn't that feel great to be free from the mental weights and cares that have us clogged up and bogged down?

REAL WOMAN LIFE NUGGET:
Real *women keep their inner houses clean, swept, carefree and focused on what really matters the most every day of their lives!*

"...Let us lay aside every weight, and the sin which so easily ensnares us, and let us run with endurance the race that is set before us... "
Hebrews 12:1

Get that. It is our job *daily* to lay aside weights and sin that is designed to ensnare, trap and keep us from running with endurance our life's race. We can't run as swiftly with shackles on. Daily cleansing of our hearts and souls through prayer to God is good practice because it keeps us free to run. One of the benefits of prayer is emptying our hearts of its cares. This emptying of everything that is on our hearts is the way that God has designed our daily living. Life just won't be as difficult to run everyday if we begin practicing this principle...it works!

"Trust in Him at all times, you people, pour out your heart before Him, God is a refuge for us."
Psalm 62:8.

The only person in this universe that can make everything all right is GOD. He's our refuge, our hiding place. We must trust Him enough to pour out your heart to him, because He and He alone is always there and cares for us at all times. Don't be foolish enough to think, "I can handle my problems and concerns." We can't! God is the only One Who is able to do something with and about our cares. We must lay aside daily, moment-by-moment, weights and sin that are designed to trap us in mental turmoil. Our job is to lay the stuff down. God's job is to remove it far, far away from us and refresh, renew and re-ignite our lives. We've cleared one hurdle, now let's move deeper into an important step, knowing ourselves.

Step Two: Knowing
"Before I formed you in the womb I knew you; Before you were born I sanctified you; I ordained you"
Jeremiah 1:5

Ever felt all alone, like no one else on the planet knew you or what was going on with you? I've discovered in life, that in and of myself, I really don't have the power to know me. Unless I have the courage to go back to my Maker, and allow Him the pleasure of telling me about me, I've discovered, I will never reach my full potential. God and God alone *knows* me and you.

Envision the artist's canvass. In the beginning it's totally blank. Then, stroke-by-stroke, colors, life, shapes, thoughts, feelings and emotions spill onto the canvass creating a beautiful picture with depth and height and meaning and substance. Great beauty spills from the artist's head and heart until finally the masterpiece is complete and it's a wonder for the world to behold and enjoy. This is God's design of us.

He started with a blank canvass. But methodically, carefully, thoughtfully, each brush stroke created brilliance, excellence, temperament, personality, skin tone, thoughts, desires, purpose, destiny, hopes, dreams, loves, dislikes, body type, hair length until finally the creation—YOU— were complete and then impregnated into your mother's womb!

God has said that before you ended up in your mother's womb He knew you. This word "knew" means to know by *seeing*. God saw you before you were in your mother's womb. He saw your end. He wrote the script of your life, your husband, your children, your purpose, your destiny. He saw your ups and downs, ins and outs, falls and triumphs! He saw you, your body, your hair, your smile, your eyes. He created the exact masterpiece that He wanted a relationship with. That masterpiece is you.

It stands to reason that in God's infinite wisdom, He hid uniqueness, exquisiteness, unseen depths within each created woman that He reserved to tell us about Himself. God is waiting to reveal to you and me all that we ever wanted to know about ourselves. He knows our purpose, our destiny and the life He wants us to have. He knows why He created you, what He had in mind when He created you. We just need to come to the conclusion that He alone is able to heal and fix you everywhere you hurt and are broken.

"Eye has not seen, nor ear heard, nor have entered into the heart of man the things which God has prepared for those

> *who love Him. But God has revealed them to us through His*
> *Spirit. For the Spirit searches all things,*
> *yes, the deep things of God."*
> *1 Corinthians 2:9-10*

What an awesome thought! No one's eyes except God's eyes and no one's ears except God's ears and no one's heart except God's heart has seen, heard or knows all that He has prepared for me and you. But God is waiting and willing to reveal those things to us through His Spirit in our times of intimacy with Him. That is mind-blowing.

Come up higher ladies! We are missing some *awesome* stuff messing around with petty little things. Our abundant lives are waiting for us in God and it's time we go get them!

God is the only one who can fix what's wrong with you, or help you discover who you really are! God and God alone can tell you why you do what you do. He is able to help you to know you. Don't overlook this step. In the search for self, in the journey of becoming a real woman, asking God for His help and input is a vital part.

Who else but the manufacturer of your soul can tell you why you feel what you feel? Who else can help you determine what's best for you, which way to turn, or how to respond to life? Have you asked God who to marry, where to live or what career choice to make? Do you know for sure that in the script for your life that business deal you are about to engage in should exist? Are you sure you are living where it's best for you and for your children? Real women have the realization that without Christ they can do nothing, but through Him, we becoming overcomers and super achievers in life!

Step Three: Transparency and Intimacy

Transparency and intimacy are where you begin this step of knowing yourself. If we approach this *process* (and trust me it is a process!) as real women, free from pretense, not being phony or deceptive, being frank and honest with ourselves, we are ready to begin.

Intimacy with God is the vehicle for transparency. Think of intimacy as *"see-into-me."* By asking God to look into us, behind the hurts, pains, frustrations, thoughts and feelings, we become open to receive all of Him. If we allow intimacy to take place between our Heavenly Father and ourselves, we are well on our way towards knowing ourselves in real ways that we have never dreamed of. God plays His part in revealing to us "the good, the bad and the ugly" about us and we do our part in pulling down all defenses and all selfish motives, leaving our hearts and souls transparent and open before the Lord through intimacy with Him.

He holds all the secrets as to how you can create the kind of life worth living! Bottomline: God can reveal to you who you really are!

Selah, Pause, Think and TAKE ACTION
Getting To Know You... Transparency!

GET REAL! Who are you really? Your character or the type of person you are, is who you are when no one else is around. Are you really a liar, a cheater, a manipulator? Are you trustworthy, dependable, or are you manipulative and deceitful? Are you a woman of morals and principles? Are you a holy and godly woman?

Without deceiving yourself, but becoming honest, frank and free from pretense, describe below who you are right now in your life and jot down how you feel about yourself. *(i.e., I'm a 36-year-old woman who struggles with discontentment. Overall life is good for me now, but I am striving to get my attitude, anger and frustration under control. I am happy and content with me right now, but I want more...I recognize I need God's help...)*

A real woman knows herself. I am:

_____

_____

_____

Re-establishing, finding or knowing the real you also includes becoming familiar with your needs and desires. Since far too many women spend most or all of our time meeting the needs of others, we easily lose touch with one of the most important relationships of all—the relationship with ourselves.

Take a moment to re-connect with you. Answer the following: What is the one thing you have always secretly desired or dreamed about (be specific)?

_____

_____

_____

Have you obtained or are you currently striving toward this desire or dream?_____

If not, why have you given up or lost hope concerning it?

_____

_____

RECAP

There is power in being a Real woman. There is happiness when you are a woman who is not artificial, not a fraud, but who is genuine and lives the "what you see is what you get" lifestyle. There is stability in being a Real woman. There is benefit in being a Real woman. You can bank on boosting your confidence, self-esteem and value to yourself and the world when you live the life of being a Real woman.

Don't forget:
- Being real starts with finding and knowing the Real you.
- Finding and knowing yourself requires you to daily pour out your heart before the Lord; empty your heart of all its cares.
- Knowing yourself is a life-long process and it begins with being transparent with yourself and before God.
- Transparency operates safely through intimacy with God. Asking Him to *see-into-me!*

My personal definition of what it means to be a _Real_ woman is:

_____

31

The Power Of Being A <u>Real</u> Woman

Have I been a <u>Real</u> woman?_____

What things can I do right now to start being <u>Real</u>? _____

_____

_____

Personal Thoughts:

CHAPTER TWO

The _Real_ Me I Want The World To See

_"...But a woman who fears the Lord, she shall be praised...
let her own works praise her in the gates."_
Proverbs 31:30-31

Now that we have a real, honest foundation to spring board from, let's take some of the information we've digested and learn how to apply it to our lives.

Are you beginning to discover that this process of becoming a _Real_ woman, although uncomfortable, can leave you with a feeling of accomplishment? Are you beginning to see that you really were lost or buried or bruised or maybe bits and pieces of your life had begun to slip away?

It can be shocking to realize that you have fallen asleep on your life. Many of us fail to take heed or wake up to the fact that this is the only life we will ever have and it worth living if we take the time to take care of it! If we don't wake up, our own lives will simply pass us by.

The _Real_ women that we are becoming will reward us with the praises of loved ones, peers, and friends in the important places and times of our lives. This is what Proverbs is talking about when the virtuous woman is told she will be praised if she fears and respects the Lord and does her part in making sure her life is in order through an understanding and knowledge of herself. Then the works that she does will be recognized and praised by everyone who comes in contact with her.

Question: Whatever Happened To The _Real_ Me?

Where am I? Where was I? What had or has me distracted? What was keeping me blocked from allowing God to see into me? Why was I phony? Why did I become artificial? What makes it difficult for me to show to others who I really am? These are some profound life-changing questions that at various times in your life throughout your days you need to ask yourself and answer.

We can't live life without sharing our lives with others. Life is only worth living when we can break who we are and feed our real selves to those in our lives and spheres of influence. We can't have real relationships even with our husbands and children or our families and friends if we've not truly begun a life-long process of cultivating transparency or in other words commit to being Real all the time!

Cultivating Transparency

Our goal should be to allow people to see what is in our heart. Do your children know who you really are? Or do you pretend to be the "all knowing," "always right," Mom? Does your husband know your heart, your dreams, and your desires? Do you allow true girlfriends the ability to see who and what you are on the inside? It's time to take another important step in becoming a Real woman. It's time to learn how to take off the mask!

Becoming "maskless" is probably the scariest determination and move that we can make as human beings.

Becoming maskless is a three-fold process:

1. **I take off my mask to myself.** No more lying to myself. No more self-deception. I must be and remain honest with me all the time.

2. **I take off my mask to God.** Lord, here I am, good, bad and ugly, check me out. I give you permission to see me naked. Do you want to know something? Nothing about you surprises God and there is nothing about you that God hasn't already considered! This is an awesome thought: nothing surprises Him, nothing scares Him away and there is nothing that He hasn't already considered about you and has chosen to love you anyway!

3. **I can then take my mask off to others.** After being real with myself and with my God, it's so simple to take the next step of taking my mask off to others. At this point you can conclude, if you are okay with yourself and okay with your God, what can others do to you? If God is for us, who can be against us and who can have any effect on our lives?

When are we going to realize as women and as people that transparency=authenticity? Authentic men and women in this day and age are rare, few and far between. When we meet real, authentic people, we don't even know how to respond to them. We find ourselves saying, "Is she for real?" We balk in disbelief. Yet, this is the true life of a Godly woman. She must be authentic, tried and proven over the years. Her "yes" must mean yes and her "no" must mean no. She upholds integrity and morality like beacons in the darkness. She is committed to living out her life openly and transparently before others because she realizes that transparency and genuineness alone strip others of their defenses and allow love and warmth to flow from her life into the lives of those she cares for.

Now of course there is balance here. Use transparency with much wisdom and deliberation. Don't blindly go about opening your heart and soul, the core of who you are, to everyone you come in contact with. But when you engage in a relationship, risk intimacy and transparency when you feel it is appropriate. I say "risk," because you're vulnerable and open to hurt or disappointment, but Jesus is always there to help in difficult times. He has your back no matter what!

Letting Go... To Become The Woman I Want To Be

You want to know the greatest secret about going on and up to the next level in your life: <u>Forgetting everything that is behind!</u> Yesterday is truly over. We all need to appreciate and accept the women we are growing to be by choosing to let go of our past. This includes our old ways of thinking.

Wherever you are in life, whatever stage or season, acceptance of where you are is vital to your survival. This is called being content. Being *content* for some of us is a serious struggle (both of my hands are raised high!). Some of us just are never satisfied. We want better cars, bigger houses, smarter, more well-behaved children, adoring husbands, high paying jobs and on and on. But at the core of all of these desires (which are not bad, by the way) is this nagging feeling of frustration, anger, negativity and things never being good enough where we are.

To be content is to *limit oneself in requirements, desires or actions*. It simply means to put the brakes on the resentment we carry and feel about what we currently have or where we currently are in life. I can desire a bigger house, but I should not despise the one I currently have. While I'm training my children's bad behavior now so that they can become better people, I should recognize the good in them now too, so I won't become discouraged with them. While I may secretly desire to have an adoring, affectionate, passionate, husband, I must realize that if I encourage, respect, appreciate and admire who my husband is right now, right where he is at, my life with him will become much better. He may never change, but I can change and grow to love him more.

RECAP

If we truly want praise and blessing in our lives from others around us, we should strive towards the goal of being the best ME possible. Being a real woman requires waking up to our lives, realizing that just like we put deodorant on every day, we need to work on the hidden woman of our hearts everyday. Staying connected with her, knowing her hopes, fears and hidden agendas. We should cultivate transparency and work on taking the mask off with ourselves, with our God and with our loved ones.

Don't forget:
- Transparency=Authenticity. Strive to be a real, transparent, authentic woman of God every day.
- Becoming "maskless" is scary but necessary to be a successful genuine woman.
- Take the mask off to yourself. Don't be deceived!

- Take the mask off with God. Allow Him to see into you.
- Take the mask off with close relationships and friends. Dare to risk intimacy and closeness with others through being Real…they'll love you for it!

Personal Thoughts:

CHAPTER THREE

The Whole Woman, Free to Soar Again

"...they shall mount up with wings like eagles..."
Isaiah 40:31

So we've started the journey toward change. We've discovered some valuable nuggets about the power of being a _Real_ woman, but we still aren't "there" yet.

We've begun to get the rumblings and stirrings of hope that things can and will be better, but we recognize that we still have work to do. What's next? Glad you asked. Next, is soaring!

If we want to soar, we must begin with attempting to get whole.

"But those who wait on the Lord shall renew their strength; they shall mount up with wings like eagles, they shall run and not be weary, they shall walk and not faint."
Isaiah 40:31

Just think about it...

Soaring like an eagle!
Running and not growing weary!
Walking and not fainting! How can this be? What do we need operating in our lives to make this happen? Well it

goes back to where we began this journey…with our thoughts in our mind. We must change our mind-set toward difficulties, situations and circumstances that will come at us in life. In case you haven't realized it yet, life is hard sometimes and it just stinks sometimes. But how we respond will determine our ability to stay real and to soar high above the "stinky" parts of life!

We can use the "turbulence" of life to actually lift us higher when we are operating on a higher level. We must learn to keep focused and see something!

"While we do not look at the things which are seen, but at the things which are not seen…"

What Do You See?

We must understand that the life that is lived out in front of us consists of a whole bunch of stuff that is temporary.

Temporary means *lasting for a limited time*. See, we get worked up, stressed out, and overcome by stuff that will only last for a limited time! Understand the Bible is saying that hard times are limited based upon the measuring stick of eternity. What's six months of bad stuff when you have eternity to measure it against? What's bankruptcy, sickness or distress for periods of time when you think about the fact that we will live forever?

But there is a key to the limited time: we must be looking at the "things" which are not seen with our natural eyes. If we continue (as most of us do) wallowing and smothering ourselves with our here and now full of trouble, confusion and mess from other people, then we will never be able to soar!

We must become women of vision that see things that nobody else can see. My purpose, my destiny, the wonderful plans and purposes that God has in store for me! I'm able to overcome and endure my life, when I am holding on to the "unseen" victories, the unseen accomplishments, the unseen greatness that is yet to come for me.

One stepping stone in mastering becoming a visionary in order to soar is prioritizing you!

Step One To Soar
Learning How To Prioritize My Life—
Write the Vision

It will help you to see on paper what you "see" with your inner eye of faith.

"Write the vision and make it plain on tablets, that he may run who reads it. For the vision is yet for an appointed time; but at the end it will speak, and it will not lie. Though it tarries, wait for it; because it will surely come, it will not tarry."
Habakkuk 2:2-3

Yes, Lord!

Selah...Pause, Think and TAKE ACTION
Write the Vision

- Write the vision
- Make it plain
- The vision is for an appointed time
- Wait for it

Vision is a fascinating thing. The Bible says,
"Where there is no revelation (prophetic vision) the people
cast off restraint; but happy is he who keeps the law."
Proverbs 29:18

In essence if we don't see something, our lives will be
undisciplined, unfruitful and unproductive.

But before we talk about the grandiose "Vision for our
lives...destiny and purpose..." let's talk about the small
seemingly mundane "visions" or goals that we can use as
marks or guideposts along the way to move our lives along.
I realize that many women can't even fathom a "destiny" yet,
because life has rocked and rolled for so hard and for so
long, that we are just trying to get stable. With this in mind,
let's talk about being visionaries on a day-to-day basis.

Maybe your vision for yourself is as simple as to quit
smoking, or to quit cussing, lying or manipulating people.
Maybe you need to see yourself driving a new car, living in a
new home or having all of your bills paid. You could even
have a vision for reaching a lost and dying world, helping
women and ministering to others! One word of advice...*take
care and make sure that your own house is in order before
you venture into a "cleaning service" for other people,
helping them!*

With this said, write a plain and simple vision here:

_____

_____

Step Two To Soar
Prioritizing Your Life!

It might help in vision planning/writing if we were to also have our priorities for our lives readily available. What are your "set in stone" priorities? What is superior in rank, position or privilege in your life? Are your children your priority? Is your husband your priority? Most importantly is your relationship with the Lord your priority? Priorities are crucial to our success. Some things must take precedence and priority over other things. With this said, let's list our priorities. I'll use mine as an example. You see without these set in stone elements my life will take on its own life and leave me slave to a demanding schedule, frustration and aggravation. My priorities are simple:

1. GOD (My intimate relationship with Him)
2. MY FAMILY (My intimate relationship with Tony and Morgan, Naomi, Caleb and Samantha)
3. MY CAREER/CALLING (Today's Black Woman Corp. and everything else)

This is simple…it keeps me on track and every decision I make I try my best to filter through these priorities…Is this okay Lord? How will this affect my children? Would Tony (my husband) approve of this? Am I remaining true to the call of God on my life and my career? It makes decision making a lot easier. Now, what are your top three priorities:

Selah…Pause, Think and TAKE ACTION
Establish the boundaries—Setting Priorities

1. _____

2. _____

43

3. _____

Step Three To Soar
Expansion—Prudently!

_"She considers a new field before she buys or accepts it—
expanding prudently and not courting neglect of her present
duties by assuming other duties—with her savings of time
and strength, she plants fruitful vines in her vineyard."_
Proverbs 31:16 amplified

Now that we have our vision written, and our priorities established, we can learn how to add to our lives "stuff" that comes up on a daily basis.

To be prudent is _having the ability to govern and discipline oneself by the use of reason;_ it's marked by wisdom, and it's being shrewd in the management of practical affairs.

In this plan to becoming whole and being a _Real_ woman, we must consider one crucial principle: we can't add anything to our lives without thought about the overall picture.

A wise woman considers before she buys or accepts anything into her life. To consider implies forethought, deep thought before making commitments or accepting whatever comes your way. That includes negativity from well-meaning people, sickness and disease that tries to eat away at your body or even the food you're about to put into your mouth...consider the cost before buying!

Too many times as women we find ourselves burdened down doing a lot of things that we don't have the time to do or even want to do. We're having our glory and excellence stolen from us through over commitment and disorganized lives. We can't shine and we can't soar like this! Remember, without vision, without seeing where you are going your life will veer off on its own course and you'll find yourself in a ditch on the side of the road.

Expanding your life is a must, but this should be done with wisdom, shrewdness, discipline and reasonable management. Don't say yes just because it's expected! By the same token, don't drag your feet when it's time to act and move. Expand your life, and the borders of your life with thought and care.

Expansion must also take place with your current duties, assignments and commitments taken under consideration. How will this affect my husband? My children? My job? What are my current responsibilities? Is this what you want me to do Lord? See we're not thinking! Most of us are not assessing situations based on our current configuration of life…we're just floating and existing and adding on a whim!

The Bible promises that if we will expand with wisdom that we will automatically engage in a "savings of time." What, a savings of time? How many of you feel that you actually have a savings of time at the end of the day, week or year? This can happen if we will begin to have the soaring mentality and will determine that we want to be whole so we can SOAR! With that savings of time the wise woman is able to "plant fruitful vines in her vineyard."—the vineyard of your children's lives, your husband's life, your colleagues' lives. Being able to use your savings of time and your extra strength to plant vines of health, happiness and blessings into the lives of those you touch and love. This is an awesome thought! If I do my part and expand prudently, and don't neglect my present duties, then I will save my time and strength and I will be able to plant good vineyards into the lives of those who are nearest and dearest to me! This is an awesome promise and you can bet this will allow us to soar way above the mundane, messy lives we've settled for.

Step Four To Soar
Overcoming the enemies to your soul— idleness, and self-pity!

"She looks well to how things go in her household, and the bread of idleness— gossip, discontent and self-pity, she will not eat."
(Proverbs 31:27)

Do you know that idle means *lacking worth or basis; useless, not occupied, having no employment,* and *to run disconnected so that power is not used for useful work.* Whew! Please don't be a woman who is lacking worth or who is useless. When we are not occupied with a vision for seeing ourselves blessed of God, we can easily fall into this state of being "unemployed" in life with no purpose, nothing to do or nothing to look forward to. Our goal in soaring is to be able to utilize all of our power, energy, creativity and strength at full force to accomplish the goals and objectives set before us! Raising children, running a household, caring for our husbands, having meaningful friendships and relationships and then ultimately touching our world!

Now, let's talk about self-pity. It will suffice to say, no more pity parties! Learn to encourage yourself. If there is no choir of support and everybody has left you to die...learn to make your soul shut up and look up to where your strength is coming from.

"Why are you cast down (bowed down), O my soul? And why are you disquieted within me? Hope in God, for I shall yet praise Him for the help of His countenance."
Psalm 42:5

In essence, the psalmist David asked himself, what is wrong with me...hope in God! See what God is going to do...see what my life in Him is going to be when this situation passes. It's always darkest at midnight...but the morning is coming. No more self-pity!

FREEDOM! Learning To Let Go and Say No

Freedom is a wonderful thing. In this next section we are going to go through a major overhaul using as our checklist the definition of freedom. We're going to dig deep and discover the weights, sin and encumbrances that have us grounded and keep us from flying!

Selah...Pause, Think and TAKE ACTION
Moving toward freedom

Our self-discovery should never end. Let's keep it Real and use the following checklist to see the areas where our lives have become "grounded." Please read the following list and check any area(s) that apply to you.

_____ Imprisoned (Are you being held captive by negative attitudes, bad relationships or anything that is proving harmful to your life?)

____ Enslaved (Are you a slave to alcohol, relationships, sex, drugs, lying, stealing or any other vice?)

____ At liberty (Are you free from the inside-out?)

____ Controlled by obligation or the will of another (Do you feel like someone else is controlling your life negatively?)

____ Free from want in my life (Are you free from any lack in your life?)

____ Free from need in my life (Are you "need-free" meaning you have no outstanding things that you think or feel you need to make your life complete?)

____ Free from jealousy

____ Free from hatred

____ Free from anger

____ Free from sexual bondage

____ Clear (Are you able to "see" clearly with the eyes of your heart God's plan, vision and purpose for your life?)

____ Untangled (Is your life simple, non complicated and flowing smoothly?)

____ Unobstructed (Is your view from the vantage point of soaring above your circumstances?)

____ Free from burdens (Have you taken Jesus' easy yoke and light burden upon your life?)

___ Free from oppression (Do you feel free from oppressive pressure?)

___ Free from depression (Are you free from depression or depressing thoughts?)

___ FREE FROM MY PAST (This is the biggie... Are you still in bondage to your past?)

Let Go and Let God have His way!

1. FORGET
2. REACH
3. PRESS

This is the only way to move forward after you have a vision tucked away in your heart. You have to Forget the past, Reach forward toward your goal along the way, and Press as hard and as strong as you can to inch forward. Daily, hourly, minute-by-minute, life will demand that you forget what just happened, focus on what's ahead, reach for it and press toward it with all your might!

The past is no longer current, it's gone by. We use it as historical reference, but not as the determinant of our "expected end." What are you expecting for yourself? Your past can't determine that unless you let it. I don't care what you did, what they said, or what cards life dealt you, God and God alone should have the final say as to your outcome:

"For I know the thoughts that I think toward you, says the Lord, thoughts of peace and not of evil, to give you a future and a hope." Jeremiah 29:11

This should be what you see. This will allow you to soar above your past. God's thoughts about you should excite and motivate you toward His love and greatness in your life!

Now let's talk about...
SOARING!

Now that we've delved into ourselves just a little bit deeper, it's much easier to begin seeing where we need to improve. We should all have as our goal the state of being whole. We should never settle for being divided, we should strive to be healthy: spirit, soul and body! We then must commit to staying free. Free from vices, addictions, attitudes or our past. We are women of vision with purpose reaching forward toward what lies ahead. And finally, these steps enable us to begin to SOAR!

Soaring is that place of rising up. It's flying; it's gliding high with little effort, and it's to rise suddenly above the normal or accustomed level. I don't care if everyone else in your family didn't do it...you can be the first one to SOAR. You can rise above what everyone's low expectation is. You can glide with little effort!

The one principle I want to leave you with as it relates to soaring is this: Soaring is utilizing ascending air current to get a heavier-than-air craft up off the ground. What do I mean? Well, our lives aren't necessarily designed to cause us to soar. Many of us did not grow up in environments in which we were taught and challenged to soar. Many of us had bad breaks: tough beginnings and harsh realities kicked us in the butt, stripped us and left us naked and abused on the ground. A true soarer uses those very things that are meant to destroy as air current to get them off the ground. The very cuss words they used to keep you down, you can choose to use to lift you higher. Remember, these afflictions are light, while we look at unseen things.

Take the adversities, the challenges, the situations and life's problems and use them to perfect in your life patience and then after patience has had its time, it will make you whole, complete and able to SOAR!

"But those who wait on the Lord shall renew their strength; they shall mount up with wings like eagles, they shall run and not be weary, they shall walk and not faint."
Isaiah 40:31

After I find myself in a mess, if I will immediately wait on the Lord to show me, direct me, guide and lead me out of every temptation, testing and trial, then my strength and endurance will be renewed. I'll be able to run and I won't get discouraged and weary and I'll be able to walk out my life without fainting. I'll be able to take the vision God has given me and I'll be able to run with it and allow it to come into being because I see that it will come in its appointed time and it won't be late.

There is power in SOARING!

In what ways have I been grounded? _____

_____

In which areas of my life have I been held down the most?

_____

_____

I must forget:_____

I must reach:_____

I must press:_____

Personal Thoughts:

CHAPTER FOUR

Relationship Savvy

Can two walk together unless they are agreed?
Amos 3:3

The current state of affairs that we find ourselves in relationships today is a mind-set that is very adversarial:

- Win or lose
- Right or wrong
- Mine or his
- Us against them

This should not be! What we truly need is to have the mind-set of unity, undivided, unbroken agreement in relationships.

Let's Get Back to the Basics!

Realize that in the course of human events and especially in our relationships, there is, according to Ecclesiastics 3:2-8, a time and a season for everything. Whether you are just starting a relationship or trying to fix one that is broken, you must realize that you are in a particular "time-frame" with that individual. Smart women always take the time to evaluate *where* they are with people they are in relationship with.

KEY RELATIONSHIP NUGGET:
The key in great relationships is to recognize/figure out the time or season that you are in with people, and what's required of you at that given moment as we allow one another the room for growth, expansion and change. Is it time to keep silent about "that issue" that you have gone over again and again with your spouse? Is it time to throw away bad attitudes and grudges? Is it time to plant some quality time with your daughter or son? Maybe it's time for peace in the family feud that has been going on for years…what time or season are you in in your relationships today?

Relationship Monster #1—SELF-SEEKING

For where envy and self-seeking exist, confusion and every evil thing are there.
James 3:16

Selfishness fueled by pride is the major destroyer of most relationships! Self-seeking is wanting the relationship on my terms, my way, in my time and wanting the other person to respond my way. Selfishness separates, destroys and creates distrust and anger between individuals.

Selah…Pause, Think and TAKE ACTION
Practical Application—What am I to do?

How to know if you are conducting yourself properly in your relationships?

1. Be honest with yourself. "But if you have bitter envy and self-seeking in your hearts, do not boast and lie against the truth." James 3:14

2.   Use this checklist from James 3:17 to see if
you're acting properly.
a. Pure. Are your motives pure?
b. Peaceable. Are you trying to keep the peace?
c. Gentle. Are you hostile or gentle?
d. Willing to yield. Have you focused on the
other person's need instead of your own?
e. Full of mercy. Are you extending mercy?
f. (Full of) good fruits. Are you blessing or
cursing the other person?

Our constant mind-set should be:

"With all lowliness and gentleness with longsuffering
bearing with one another in love, endeavoring to keep the
unity of the spirit in the bond of peace,"
Ephesians 4:2:3.

We should be long-suffering…in other words, willing to
suffer long with people, giving ample chances. We should
be endeavoring to keep unity and peace in our relationships.
Now I realize that some people are just obnoxious…but this
mandate is as much for your own peace of mind as it is for
them! We should always be striving for understanding rather
than being right in our relationships. Remember it always
takes TWO to fight, argue, bicker and throw fits. If you
change your mind and decide I am going to endeavor to keep
unity and peace and I am going to suffer longer with this
person's attitude and behavior, because I value the
relationship more than being right…your behavior will cause
automatic response and change in the other person!

KEY RELATIONSHIP NUGGET:

Another key in great relationships is to remember the
following: the ending of a relationship should be better

than the beginning! Strive to have great long-lasting relationships! No more "one-night-stand" relationships— push hard for enduring, rewarding relating with those God has placed in your life.

RELATIONSHIP MONSTER #2—ANGER

> *Do not hasten in your spirit to be angry, for anger rests in the bosom of fools.*
> *Ecclesiastes 7:9*

The Bible is clear, and I'm sure our experience has proved that:

> *"A quick-tempered man acts foolishly..."*
> *Proverbs 14:17.*

When we are easily upset and fretful, you can bet our behavior and words become irrational and out of control. So what are we to do?

Selah...Pause, Think and TAKE ACTION
Practical Application—What am I to do?

James 1:19
Let every man (every person) be:

1. SWIFT to hear...

2. SLOW to speak...

3. SLOW to wrath...

Be willing to HEAR what's truly being said first. Be slow to RESPOND BACK to what is being said. Be slow to GET ANGRY and blow up.

FOUNDATIONS OF PEACEFUL LIVING

Here's another quick checklist for you to use from Ephesians 4:25-32 to keep the peace in your relationships

1. Stop lying. "...put away lying..." speak the truth only
2. Do not let the sun go down on your wrath.
3. Do not give place to the devil/evil.
4. Let no corrupt communication come out of your mouth, but what is good for necessary edification—imparting grace to the hearer.
5. Do not grieve the Holy Spirit.

Put away from you
6. Bitterness.
7. Wrath.
8. Anger.
9. Clamor (Loud quarrelling).
10. Evil speaking.
11. Malice.

These things can be handled through the character trait called SELF-CONTROL.

Personal Thoughts:

ASSESSMENT OF YOUR KEY RELATIONSHIPS

Below, grade with an A,B,C,D, or Unacceptable the key relationships in your life. Start with yourself!

	A	B	C	D	Unacceptabl
SELF*					
SPOUSE					
CHILD					
CHILD					
SIBLING					
SIBLING					
MOTHER					
FATHER					
FRIEND					
FRIEND					

* Please note that you are to grade the relationship that you have with yourself. This is crucial to relating to others!

KEY RELATIONSHIP NUGGET:
You can't have a thriving relationship without self-sacrifice. (Note we are NOT saying you must stay in physically abusive situations!) Relationships can and will cost you something—in the "better" relationships it will cost you EVERYTHING! The "everything" that you give up will be your thinking, your ways, and your will "given up" for the relationship so that it can thrive and grow!

Normally human nature:
1.   DEFENDS itself.
2.   EXCUSES itself.
3.   JUSTIFIES itself.
4.   EXALTS itself.
5.   PROTECTS itself.
AT ALL OTHERS' EXPENSE!

We will NOT have thriving relationships this way—WE MUST CHANGE!

1.   RETHINK our positions.
2.   RE-DEFINE the terms and meanings of relationships.
3.   RE-EDUCATE ourselves about Christian principles and relating.
4.   RE-EVALUATE our current state of affairs—are we truly relating successfully?
5.   REJOICE! A new day is dawning!

KEY RELATIONSHIP NUGGET
Master the art of empathy. Learn to look at life from the other person's vantage point. Walk in their shoes. Empathize, feel what they feel. For most of us it may be difficult to do this when we are extremely close to the other

person. But for greater understanding with people we love, don't just stop at seeing their point of view; go beyond to actually feel what they feel.

Decide today that you want better relationships and decide that you are going to do things correctly to make them happen.

Developing successful relationships starts with:

1. A DECISION, then you add
2. A PLAN, then you embark on the journey of
3. CHANGE

Selah...Pause, Think and TAKE ACTION
Practical Application—What am I to do?

Let's decide to change our relationships right now. The journey toward success starts with you, depends on you and ends with you! Not the other person...YOU!

1. THE DECISION

I am going to work on my relationship
with:_____.

_____

2. THE PLAN

I am going to work on these areas within me to make things better:

_____

_____

_____

_____

3.   CHANGE, a journey!

I understand that this will take time, but I am determined to make it happen!

Matters of the Heart
Connecting Deeper In Your Relationships

Your heart represents the real you and all that you are. I have an important question for you: Who do you safely trust with your heart—knowing that they will not try to intentionally break it?

Do your children trust you with their heart? When you have been entrusted with your children's heart (and you should know) they will be vulnerable to you and share with you the deep hurts, the pains, the joy and the happiness…in essence they will share the total of who they are without reserve…the good, bad and ugly, if you have been entrusted with their heart.

Do you trust your mate with your heart? Does he/she trust you wholeheartedly? Once again, you'll know that you have heart-connected when there is a vulnerability and intimacy that allows for the free flow of sharing and information good, bad or ugly!

THE KEY INDICATORS OF SAFELY TRUSTING SOMEONE:

1. Free unhindered, unchecked sharing and talking. You don't have to watch what you say.
2. You can be you. You can relax confidently knowing that you'll be accepted and respected.
3. Nothing is too trivial or too deep to discuss. All conversation is welcomed.
4. You don't ever wonder, "Who else is going to know?"
5. You don't have to work at enjoying their presence—instead you're looking for ways to be with the person. Relating with them is NOT a chore.
6. You respect what they say and over time you willingly conform to any suggestions or corrections they make.
7. You reveal your hurt and pain.
8. You reveal your joy, good news and excitement.

Selah...Pause, Think and TAKE ACTION
More Practical Application—What I can do!

1. Learn to focus on your feelings, response, position and responsibility in the relationship, instead of always looking at the other person and their behavior.
2. Learn better communication skills that allow you the flexibility of talking to others in a way that they understand from their point of view what you are saying. Talk the way they hear.
3. Allow time to heal wounds that have been created...the current and the past.

4. Practice forgiveness. Practice these phrases: please forgive me, I forgive you, I was wrong and I'm sorry.

5 Damaging Myths About Forgiveness

I had an interview for my radio show with Robert Jeffress, author of the book, *When Forgiveness Doesn't Make Sense.* He gave me the most practical perspective and advice for my listening audience that I had ever heard about the subject of forgiveness. Let's take a look at the five damaging myths about forgiveness.

- **Forgiveness should only happen if the offending individual shows remorse.** *Forgiveness releases you. It frees you from the bondage of being attached to the offender. You do not have to have the other person's "I'm sorry," before you decide to release them from the penalty of what they did to you.*

- **True forgiveness means that the offending party should be released from the consequences of his or her actions.** *The Bible is clear, "Do not be deceived, God is not mocked; for whatever a man sows, that he will also reap," Galatians 6:6. When you "sow" offense into a person's life, without true repentance, EXPECT to reap what you have sown. Although the offended person may forgive the person who commits a crime against them, the offender still has to face the legal ramifications of the crime and still may find themselves suffering the consequences of their actions.*

- **True forgiveness means that the forgiver should re-establish a relationship with the**

offending person. *You do NOT have to re-establish a relationship with a person who has wronged you after you have forgiven them. End of discussion...life can go on.*

- **True forgiveness means that the forgiver must also forget what was done**. *It does not mean that you have not forgiven if you still remember what was done to you. You are built and designed with memory recall (per God's design!). You will remember, vividly, what was done to you. As time heals, the pain associated will diminish and the wounds will scab over, but you may never forget. This DOES NOT mean that you have not forgiven. Remember, forgiveness is relinquishing your "right for vengeance and retaliation" against someone who has done you wrong.*

- **There are some crimes, offenses or other things that people can do to one another that can never be forgiven**. *What has the Lord forgiven you from? There is no sin so great that can't be eradicated by the blood of Jesus Christ! We must never forget this!*

Selah...Pause, Think and TAKE ACTION
Practical Application—Don't Be Critical

- Don't jump on one another's failures
- Don't criticize one another's faults
- Don't have a critical spirit
- Do recognize your own faults and failures so you won't be concerned about other's faults
- Don't play a holier-than-thou role in the lives of those around us

WHAT IS THE CURE FOR A CRITICAL SPIRIT?
It's the PEACE of the Lord!

Stop allowing yourselves to be agitated and disturbed; and do not permit yourselves to be fearful and intimidated and cowardly and UNSETTLED. We are so easily offended because we allow ourselves to be open and unguarded. The bible says to guard your heart, because your very life flows from within you. We do not interface with one another from positions of peace; we fellowship and interface with one another from positions of neediness...and as soon as we fail to meet one another's needs, we are offended and are caused to stumble.

Let's strive to bring the decency and order back into our lives and the lives of those we care deeply about.

What key areas do I need to work on in improving my significant relationships?

_____

_____

_____

Am I really judgmental and critical of others? _____

Personal Thoughts:

Personal Thoughts:

CHAPTER FIVE

Empowered Singles, Thriving In The New Millennium

Today's Single Woman must be empowered:

1. Spiritually (in her heart)
2. Emotionally (in her mind, and emotions)
3. Physically (in her body)
4. Financially (in her pocketbook)
5. Relationally (in her significant relationships)

So let's find out how to make this happen, beginning with defining single. Single means *consisting of a separate unique, whole individual, unbroken or undivided.*

A single person is a separate, unique, whole individual. He or she is unbroken and undivided. By this definition, we could say that every human being on the planet is truly single. We are all separate, unique and whole individuals. We all should be unbroken and undivided in our relationship with the Lord.

Unfortunately, we have gone to such great lengths in categorizing and labeling people that we have managed to alienate a good number of people. Because we have failed to look at the totality of the definition of single, we have reduced the definition of singleness to simply unmarried people. While that is partly true, being single is so much more! And I might add it is that place we ALL must strive to get to!

Picking apart the definition:

Beginning at the beginning, what does it really mean to be single? Let's take a closer look at the definition.

Separate: to set or keep apart.

Today's Christian single is to be first and foremost, (like all Christians) set apart.

"And do not be conformed to this world, but be transformed by the renewing of your mind..."
Romans 12:2a

Empowerment or being empowered simply translated means being blessed...***being empowered to prosper*** (which is the definition of bless)! As today's Christian Single you must determine that you will remain separate from the world. Separate from the world's ways of thinking, acting, socializing and living. I want to make sure that you understand that this mandate to "be separate" is the same mandate that married people have. You are no different because you are asked to be separate! As a successful Christian single, you must determine to remain set apart, being separate from anything that will draw you away from being the best that God has designed for you to be.

Unique: being the only one, very rare or uncommon.

Ladies and gentlemen, you are the only one like you! You are very rare or uncommon in the sense that God

Himself crafted, designed and molded you into the individual that you are!

"Before I formed you in the womb, I knew you; before you were born I sanctified you..."
Jeremiah 1:5a

God said, before you were ever placed inside your mother's womb, He already had an intimate knowledge of you. He already sanctified or set you apart for relationship with Him. God already predetermined that you would enter into this world a separate, unique individual. This is His plan for every human being on the planet!

I want you to begin to see the larger picture about "singleness." Singleness should not only be a term used to describe someone who isn't married...it is the empowering blessing of the Lord upon every individual on the planet. We are all empowered, called, anointed and appointed to be single, separate, unique and whole! It is God's power working in us to be unique, and separate, set apart for relationship with the Lord. And set apart to fulfill our own individual destinies and purposes.

Whole: free of wound or injury, free of defect or impairment; physically sound and healthy; having all its proper parts or components; complete; an undivided unit.

WOW! What a definition! As single individuals we should be (and are created to be) FREE from wound or injury, FREE from defect or impairment, physically sound and healthy and get this: We have all of our proper parts or components; we are undivided.

"Now may the God of peace Himself sanctify your completely; and may your whole spirit, soul and body be preserved blameless at the coming of the Lord Jesus Christ."
2 Thessalonians 5:23

The empowerment process God is giving us here is the ability to be separate and to have our whole beings (spirit, soul and body) preserved until the Lord comes back to get us! What a promise as singles! We can be free from the injuries of our past. We can be free from "defects" in our personality like a bad temper or bad attitude. We can be physically sound and healthy in our bodies and in our emotions. We can be comfortable in our singleness, because we can relax in the fact that we have everything that we need to be complete and happy already, even without being "attached" to someone.

Too many singles feel "incomplete" without a marriage partner. This is a lie! You are created having all the parts and components that you need to function your entire life without being married. For that not to be so, it would mean that God has somehow made a mistake in designing mankind. I know that is not true; God doesn't make mistakes. So get happy sweetheart…you are whole as today's single and that means you are sound, stable and ready to take life by storm!

Unbroken and undivided are the last two definitions we need to look at and they are important.

You are not broken. You should not be walking around broken emotionally, physically or socially. You should not be divided by cares, worries, anxieties and stress. As per the "Manufacturer's" design, you are empowered to be unbroken and undivided according to the power that should be at work on the inside of you by God.

*"Now to Him who is able to do exceedingly, abundantly
above all that we ask or think according
to the power that works in us."*
Ephesians 3:20

Let me encourage you to get into the Word of God and
find out about all the "stuff" He has waiting for you,

*"...for it is God who works in you both to will and to do for
His good pleasure."*
Philippians 2:13

Single Empowerment—Spirit, Soul and Body

- **Spiritually**, understanding the Master's plan for you
  as an individual, then using all of your energy to
  execute that plan in your life daily.
- **Emotionally**, keeping your emotions under control
  and healthy at all times. This demands a regime of
  honesty, humility and transparency every day of your
  life. We must be honest with where we are, and how
  we feel about ourselves and our lives.
- **Physically**, making sure that our bodies truly remain
  the temples of the Lord. With this stand, we must
  take all necessary steps to keep our bodies healthy,
  sound and free from disease, stress, worry and
  ailment.
- **Financially**, our financial houses MUST be in order!
  We are to become good stewards over the wealth that
  has been entrusted to us by our heavenly Father.
- **Relationally**, this is the biggie. As today's
  empowered single, you must realize that marriage

isn't the answer to "make you whole." By design you are already whole and complete. As a single, it should be your goal to have thriving, loving, healthy relationships and extend yourself into the lives of those around you and in your sphere of influence. The key in doing this is being grounded and secure with the fact that you are already a whole, single, separate, unique , unbroken and undivided single person!

Personal Thoughts:

CHAPTER SIX

Dating for Today's Single Woman

I know many of you sisters out there are single and waiting on that "perfect" mate sent from Father God. Fifteen years ago, I became a married woman. To this day I'm fascinated by the dating rituals and mating processes today's woman are going through. I don't want any woman who visits my site or benefits from our information to be as desperate as the women that I see all the time trying to get a man! You don't need to show your breasts, your behind, or pretend to be something you're not to "get" or attract a man.

Ladies you are by God's design, Queens! A Queen is a female monarch who rules and reigns. I want you to think about your life right now, today. Your life (good or bad) is your kingdom, and the life you have right now you are reigning over, you rule and it's the result of what kind of Queen you are. I've chosen to relinquish my kingdom to my Lord Jesus Christ, so as I stay submitted to His Lordship, I can have His results and His life, more abundantly. Praise God! If you don't like your kingdom, it's time to change. But let me preface this by saying change is expensive and it will cost you something.

Don't moan, groan and complain about your life, your lack of a companion or the condition you're in right now— let's learn how to be God's Queens by changing and let's start reigning over lives that are worth living!

73

So, you're single and you want to attract, find and keep Mr. Right. That's an ambitious goal that is achievable. But remember, Mr. Right must be a King. Queens only marry kings. So, shaky, slick-talkers have got to go. Here are some God anointed, God appointed dating principles that I'll call The Sheeba Principles that you can use to get God's results in your dating.

(This information is taken from and based on the Bible. It would help you greatly if you take the time to sit down and read the text: 1Kings 10:1-13)

Sheeba Dating Principles for Today's Single Woman

The Queen of Sheeba is one of my favorite Biblical heroines. My girl was BAD! She had it together so much she caught the eye of the richest, wisest man that ever existed in the Bible…and I don't think it's coincidental that she was a SISTER! Through her encounter with King Solomon, we can learn some important truths about our approach to men that we encounter.

First and foremost ladies, you must carry yourself as a Queen, a sovereign; a woman who is in charge, knows who she is and what she wants. Queens aren't "hoochies." Queens don't display their bodies. Queens don't use foul language, bad posture or in any way display themselves in a manner that is beneath them. Queens are not arrogant; they are gracious, kind, gentle, and generous. They are virtuous women! Read the follow list of attributes and action statements of a virtuous woman, to see how we are to conduct ourselves as Queens.

A Virtuous Woman

She is found
She is worthy
She does her husband good
She seeks wool and flax
She willingly works
She brings food from afar
She rises while it is yet night
She provides food
She considers fields for purchase
She girds herself with strength
She strengthens her arms
She perceives that her merchandise is good
She stretches out her hand to the distaff
She extends her hand to the poor
She reaches out her hands to the needy
She is not afraid
She makes tapestry
She makes linen garments and sells them
She's clothed with strength and honor
She opens her mouth with wisdom
She watches over the ways of her household
She's not idle
She's praised by her husband and family

We must settle this issue once and for all, we are virtuous women by God's design, you don't have to work this up; it's in you and if you belong to God all you must do is ask Him to help you develop the qualities He's already placed in you.

5 Things Queens Do When Dating Men (Kings)

The Queen of Sheeba <u>heard</u> about Solomon, about His reputation of being ALL THAT. She heard *about what kind of man and King people were saying he was.*

1. Ladies, a man always has a reputation. What are you *hearing* about him? Are you hearing he's a dog, he's a womanizer, he's no good? That's a good indication that you should beware! On the other hand if you are hearing things that sound too good to be true, or if you are hearing he's a nice guy, you need to be a little more inquisitive.

The Queen of Sheeba was not satisfied with HEARING what OTHERS had to say, she went to Solomon to TEST him with HARD QUESTIONS, to prove for herself whether this man was all they said he was.

2. Ladies, we are not spending enough time talking and questioning men that we meet and date, before we release our hearts to them! The Queen of Sheeba asked Solomon hard questions, and he answered ALL of them! The Bible says, *"...when she came to Solomon, she spoke with him about all that was in her heart. So Solomon answered all of her questions; there was nothing so difficult for the king that he could not explain it to her."* Solomon didn't lie, or skirt issues and questions. Ladies, understand that real kings don't skirt issues and your concerns. They answer ALL your questions. You need to be asking men hard questions, questions about his character, his vision for the future, his hopes, plans, desires, his job, where he stands with the Lord, what he does, what he likes, what he dislikes, how he got where he is, etc. Just because he looks and smells good, doesn't mean that he is genuinely good! HEAR ME PLEASE!

We are not asking the right questions that would give us the warning signs about his character, about his heart before we release all of who we are! ASK HARD QUESTIONS over a series of dates, over a long time and several encounters *before* you begin volunteering all of who you are!

The Queen of Sheeba came to King Solomon with "a very great company." She came with camels having spices, very much gold, and precious stones. Sistergirl was loaded with stuff. She realized that when you come into the presence of royalty you MUST come bearing gifts...you've got to have some stuff!

3.   Ladies, don't plan to attract KINGS when you don't have any "stuff!" What do I mean? A Queen must be complete on the inside before she is ready for a King! Her inner merchandise must be good and ready to exchange into a king's life. She must have spices, very much gold, precious stones; she must have gifts, talents, substance, she must be loaded with treasures for him to find inside her! She's got to be more than a body, a face and a smile! Spend your "single" time developing your treasure. You don't have to tell a King you're loaded...men know a loaded woman! I'm still surprised after all of these years of being married and four kids later how many men still flirt with me! But I also realize I endeavor to spend quality time with the Lord developing my treasure and I can see that men like, want and desire treasure inside a woman.

Then the Queen of Sheeba saw some things. She saw Solomon's wisdom through the STUFF that he had.

4.   The Queen of Sheeba saw the house he had built,
the food on his table, his servants, waiters, and
the servants apparel, their clothing, and she saw
the place he worshipped God. The queen was
able to see some substance in and through this
man. She saw through what he had built that he
knew himself, he was together, he had vision,
plans, abilities and he had stuff. He had a place
to live and people working under him. He also
most importantly had a place where he
worshipped God! She saw his relationship with
God through the fact that he had a place to
worship the Lord. It wasn't lip service, he had
real relationship with God! Ladies, with the men
you are dating what do you see? What do you
really see? Is he a man of influence and
substance? Is he put together? Does he have
vision? Most importantly, does he have a place, a
church that he worships God in, for himself? Is
he in relationship with the Lord already, apart
from you? Ladies, what do you see?

*When all of these things took place the Bible says the Queen
of Sheeba was satisfied: "...there was no more spirit in her."
Then she said to the king, "It was a true report which I
heard in my own land about your words and your wisdom.
However, I did not believe the words until I came and saw
with my own eyes; and indeed the half was not told me. Your
wisdom and prosperity exceed the fame of which I heard."
(1 Kings 10:5-7)*

5.   She thoroughly satisfied her own heart before
declaring that what she had heard was true. She
took her time and used her Queen's instincts and
decision-making abilities to determine that he
was truly a king and a man worth admiring.

Ladies, have you taken time with that man you think is Mr. Right? Are you thoroughly satisfied in your heart deep down? Are you absolutely sure he is all that he's represented himself to be? Don't release your heart until you are truly satisfied deep within.

Then, and only after these series of events did the Queen of Sheeba release to Solomon the "who" she was and the "what" she had. The Queen didn't hop in the bed after one dinner and a movie with Solomon. She didn't give him her body, soul and mind after one mindless conversation and a ride in an expensive car. A Queen knows and realizes her worth and she also recognizes how one "emotional fling" can leave everlasting repercussions in and on her kingdom. Only after a series of exhausting events did the Queen of Sheeba release herself to Solomon. "Then she gave the king one hundred and twenty talents of gold, spices in great quantity, and precious stones. There never again came such abundance of spices as the Queen of Sheeba gave to King Solomon." (1 Kings 10:10)

6.   Another translation of the Bible says the Queen gave him spices rare and great in quantity. Rare spices, unique spices, spices that were in such abundance that she out-gave what anyone had ever given to him. Ladies, you should be so loaded with spice, unique, valuable treasures, precious stones, rare in quality, character on the inside, charm and graciousness, kindness, pleasantries, wisdom and surprises that the King's mind would be blown away. This is what happened to Solomon—he had never seen such treasure. He respected the Queen before him. He appreciated her quality, her directness, her generosity and inquisitiveness. Kings know what

to do with Queens and how to treat Queens. What spices are you holding for your King, when God sends him? If you don't have any treasure or don't have much, don't worry, we're here to help you develop the woman God intends for you to be.

Recap:
1.   She HEARD of his reputation, his fame.
2.   She came to TEST him with HARD questions.
3.   She came with a VERY GREAT COMPANY; she came with some stuff.
4.   She SAW his wisdom, his house, his stuff.
5.   She PROVED for herself that he really was what they said he was.
6.   She then gave him out of her TREASURE great spices that were rare and unique.

Happy Dating!

Personal Thoughts:

CHAPTER SEVEN

Today's Christian Woman and Sex— Healing For Our Souls

Sex. It's not a topic discussed openly, thoroughly, and thoughtfully, like we're so in need of as women; but that's changing right here today.

You see, God knows that many of His daughters are not complete, victorious, whole sexual beings. We are incompetent, hurt, abused, trapped, frustrated, and discouraged when it comes to the subject of our sexuality, sex in our marriages, and the sexual feelings we have in our singleness. Where do we go? To whom do we turn? I've got good news for you today, His name is Jesus!

Well ladies, if you want to know what God is thinking about, I'll tell you: it's SEX! Sex is on our minds a whole lot, so you can be assured sex is on God's mind too. His intentions are to reconcile us back to Himself in the area of our female sexuality. All the past hurt, misunderstanding, loss of virginity, unfulfilled sexual relationships with our husbands, freedom from sexual sins…God fully intends to wipe the slate clean, start over in Him, and give us brand new starts!

The truth is that many of us feel impure. We love the Lord, but we're trapped by our past, our present, our addiction, our lust and we can't break free. Then there are others who simply want more, more as a woman. Then there are singles who are desperately struggling with sexual feelings and don't know what to do.

God is aware of this and He has come to help!

"Therefore say to the children of Israel: I am the Lord; I will bring you out from under the burdens of the Egyptians! I will RESCUE you from their bondage and I will redeem you with an outstretched arm..."
Exodus 6:6

We can count on His might. His power. We can look forward to God's Spirit, igniting, cleansing, restoring, removing baggage, and planting new seeds for a better tomorrow. But are we willing to "let go and let God have His way?" Do we want to do our part of separating ourselves unto Him because we love Him?

Good! Then let's get busy...

Understand ladies, *sexual intercourse*, or *copulation*, has its basic meaning, means to *fuse permanently*. Fusion takes place every time we give ourselves to a man in sexual intercourse. It's more than a man's penis entering our vagina; it's a "fusion" that is permanent! The fusion is what the Bible refers to "two flesh becoming one." I cease to be an individual in my mind, in my emotions, in my soul, when I have engaged in sexual intercourse. This needs to be emphasized because many, many, many of us are fused to men (or even women) and we don't know why we can't just *"get over them"* after the relationship is over. Our "soul" has "tied" or become one with the other person and we are fused to them permanently. It takes the work of God and God alone to unbind what has been put together through sexual intercourse.

There are so many sexual areas that we could talk about. We as women need understanding and healing in so many areas but instead of a comprehensive study of the sexual arena, I've opted to touch briefly on a few major areas that are "problem areas." I no longer wish to see women slowly die on the inside, so the silence must be broken and the enemies' strategies must be exposed. By simply defining the "issues" and realizing that the Lord wants us free from bondage, we are ready to safely move towards sexual healing and freedom.

Ready? Good, let's go!

Incest *is sexual intercourse between persons so closely related that they are forbidden, by law, to marry.* Has there been incest in your life? Has an Uncle, a cousin; a not-so-distant relative abused you sexually? Then healing is on the way!

Molestation *means to make annoying sexual advances to; it means to trouble or interfere with.* The key with molestation is that it comes with hostile intent or with intent to hurt, and harm. Were you molested as a little girl, and can't seem to break free from the fusion that took place that's haunting your life today?

Rape *is an act or instance of robbing or despoiling.* It's sexual intercourse with a woman by a man without her consent and chiefly by force or deception. Too many women have experienced rape or multiple rapes. Violation, frustration, humiliation are normal emotional responses to rape, but only the Lord can heal the broken heart and damage to your soul.

Pause to pray this prayer…

Oh Lord I need you! I need your cleansing! May your perfect will, your power to heal and your restoration strip away and make me new right now. Lord, please be with me to heal me now!

I know this may be very painful. I'm not one to dig up the past for no reason. I understand that Paul says in the Bible, "to forget those things which are behind." But God knows our frailty and our inability to break free from the traps that are meant to destroy us. He wants more than anything for us to be free!

Sadly enough, some Christian *married* women feel raped. They feel that sex with their husbands is nothing close to consensual. What do we as women do with those feelings? Of course, the woman who has experienced rape knows how hard it can be to re-establish herself as a whole, complete sexual being. Don't worry about doing it alone anymore sister, the Lord is on your side and He is here to rescue you!

Now on to more areas…

Adultery *is voluntary sexual intercourse between a married man and someone other than his wife or between a married woman and someone other than her husband.* How many broken marriages, broken hearts, broken homes have we created because of adultery? Tremendous hurt, pain and suffering can come to our hearts because of an unfaithful spouse. And yet God can restore—in fact, He wants to heal.

84

Many women turn to adulterous relationships, even Christian women, because of neglect, revenge or frustration. God says come out and be separate. He says to cleanse ourselves from adultery.

While we're on the subject, we also need to talk about adultery in our hearts. Jesus said in Matthew 15:19, *"For out of the heart proceed evil thoughts, murders, adulteries, fornications, thefts, false witness, blasphemies."* In our heart we can commit adultery against our husbands! Let me give you prime examples: soap operas! During these "flings" we fantasize, imagine, fall in love with, and are swept away with soap stars and their torrid affairs and lives time and time again. This is deception because we may then find ourselves "swept away" in our hearts by any fine, handsome figure that enters into our life. Maybe we have a crush on our pastor, a girlfriend's husband, or even a complete stranger, simply because we've opened the door. We indulge in a little harmless fantasy, or so we think, but the results can cost us our souls, our emotions, even our marriage! God says don't touch with your mind or body any unclean things or unclean thoughts. Don't "cheat" on your husband in your minds. Marriage is difficult enough!

Pornography *is the depiction of erotic behavior (as in pictures or writing) intended to cause sexual excitement.* There are a great number of homes that I know of personally that are being torn up or have been torn up by pornography. Pornography on the Internet, for example, is a trillion-dollar business. Men, and women alike are trapped by the deception of looking at naked people for the purpose of exciting ourselves sexually. As Christians, we rationalize: it's not really sex. Yes it is! The intent, our intent is what is at question here and if your intent is to cause sexual excitement for yourself, then you are on dangerous ground.

Sexual excitement, other than that found in the marriage bed, leads us into dangerous territory. How many women do you know that are torn up on the inside by husbands hooked on pornography? We're talking about Christian men! We truly need the Lord's help. Don't think this is just a man's game; women are hooked on pornography too. God wants to deliver us.

Sodomy *is anal or oral intercourse with a member of the opposite sex or intercourse with a member of the same sex or with an animal.*

I remember at one conference that I spoke at, a woman came to me with tears pouring down here cheeks afterward asking for prayer because her husband was sodomizing her against her will. As Christian married women, we know our responsibility as a wife includes sexual intercourse, but what do we do when he wants something, some technique, some style that we're not comfortable with? Does God care? Can God help? You better believe He can!

Fornication *is human sexual intercourse between unmarried people, or between a spouse and an unmarried person.* The parameters that God has set forth to play the sexual game are these: Sex can happen between two consenting adults who are married, period, END OF DISCUSSION. Married by the law of the land. Any other sexual intercourse is forbidden for the Christian woman. Why? Because God knows that sexual expression is best played out in a committed, lifelong relationship between a man and a woman committed to Christ and expressing their love for one another through sex in the marriage bed. It's for our protection. Remember what we said about sexual intercourse. It is way more than genitals meeting; it is a permanent fusion, fusing man to his woman; making the two flesh become one.

Sex is safe in a relationship that is destined for eternity. These are God's rules, not mine. If you are having sex and you are not married, STOP IT! Come out from among them and be separate, cleanse yourself, reconcile yourself back to God; He fully intends to help you today.

Homosexuality *is the manifestation of sexual desire toward a member of one's own sex; a lesbian is a female homosexual.* Flesh left to its own will seek its own pleasure; we can easily be trapped into thinking that thoughts or feelings are truth. They aren't. God's word is the only truth that the Christian need believe. Sexual feeling toward other women can be brought under subjection to the blood of Jesus, if we are willing to allow Christ to be the head in all areas of our lives. If you were caught up in homosexuality or you're struggling with the feelings, don't worry, God has shown up today to set things straight within you.

Other related sexual areas that we need healing from include:

Affairs are *romantic or passionate attachments typically of limited duration.* You know we float from one man to the next to the next feeling all the sexual tension and excitement and passion, not really committing or if we're married, cutting as close to the edge as possible to adultery. Watch out!

Flirting is when *a woman who endeavors WITHOUT SINCERE AFFECTION to gain the attention and admiration of men.* Ladies, this is fire. Check your dress, your presentation. Every woman wants the attention of men deep down but have we crossed the line? Flirting with men is a no-no especially if you know that you have no intention of becoming serious with him yet you flirt with him, making him get all hot, sweaty and bothered only to have you move to the next conquest. Come out and be separate, reconcile ourselves back to God! This is a danger-zone.

Masturbation is *a huge issue*! Studies by Christian researchers suggest that this is the biggest gray area for Christian singles and married people alike. Masturbation is erotic stimulation of the genital organs commonly resulting in orgasm and achieved by manual or other bodily contact, exclusive of intercourse, occasionally by sexual fantasies or by combinations of these agencies. What is appropriate for the Christian woman? Is masturbation allowed? I interviewed an author, Dr. William Cutrer, and I like what he said about masturbation. For the married woman it should not become the only means of reaching our climax. Mutual masturbation between married people is perfectly normal for the Christian married bed, but when masturbation, sex toys or other stimuli take the place of sexual intercourse then we run into the risk of being off kilter. Now, single Christians struggle with masturbation. Their justification for engaging in this type of erotic behavior is that they're really not engaging in sexual sin or sexual intercourse if they're by themselves, pleasuring themselves. Question? What do you think about when you engage in this activity? Jesus was clear that He expects our thoughts to be pure and holy and He expects that we will cleanse ourselves, come out and not touch unclean thoughts. Sexual arousal through the thought life and carried out through masturbation for the single Christian woman is an off-limit area. We must wait until God blesses with a spouse to fulfill our sexual needs. God is here with His grace today to help in this area of need.

Cruelty *is marital conduct which may endanger life or health or cause mental suffering or fear*. How many women are trapped in relationships where their spouse is cruel to them? This includes **physical, emotional and verbal abuse**. *Abuse is simply to attack in words, improper use or* _treatment._ Have you been abused? Or do you abuse with your mouth? Healing is available.

Last, but not least, the Lord had me add in the area of **barrenness** as it relates to our sexuality. We take for granted the fact that we are supposed to be able to bear children but, some can't. We are not able to reproduce, incapable of producing offspring but barren _also means desolate, dull and unresponsive._ These last words describe many of our sex lives with our spouses. We literally feel barren, desolate, dull, and unresponsive to him, to sex or even to the marriage. God's intent was for two people to join in this sexual union, and be fruitful. He intended for us to be able to produce fruit; fruit from sex in the form of children but also fruit in the form of enjoyment of exploration, and ecstasy in the sexual union. Orgasmic climax for women is available for those who want it! The Lord said, marriage is honorable and the marriage bed is undefiled, that means that between a husband and his wife, God says to enjoy each other thoroughly and there is nothing more wonderful than full expression between two Christian married people, exploding in their love for one another and their expression of love in Christ through love-making! God wants you restored to enjoy sex; to enjoy your sexuality and your femininity.

The Lord realizes that for many of us this work of restoration and forgiveness and cleansing will take all of His power because we simply can't do it alone.

So, where do we go from here? If you have read over these definitions and one or more areas apply to you, then you need to be FREE, whole and healed sexually. God and God alone is the healer of our broken hearts. Jesus can fix everything that is wrong with you right now. Let's see how He does it.

*...there was a woman who had a spirit of infirmity eighteen
years and was bent over and could in no
way raise herself up (straighten up).
Luke 13:10-17*

Jesus:
Saw her
Called her to Him
Said to her: woman you are loosed from your infirmity
Laid hands on her...
And immediately she was made straight and glorified God!

Then He said, "So ought not this woman; being a
daughter of Abraham, whom satan has bound, "think of it,
for 18 years, be loosed from this bond on the Sabbath?"

- Shouldn't you daughter, be loosed from the pain of
  past sexual sin? Shouldn't you, daughter, be given a
  fresh anointing from God that will re-ignite your soul
  and desire sexually for your husband?
- Shouldn't you, daughter, be able to keep yourself
  sexually pure until God blesses you with a husband?
- Shouldn't you, daughter, be free from thoughts,
  memories and the past mistakes that haunt you?
- Shouldn't you, daughter, be given the ability to soar
  to new heights of passion and sexual fulfillment with
  your husband?
- Shouldn't we all as daughters cleanse ourselves and
  come out from the world's thoughts, the world's view
  about female sexuality and sex?
- Shouldn't we separate ourselves from the world, unto
  God and give Him back our sexuality for Him to
  restore, and reconcile us?

The Lord's instruction to me was simple. He promised that His power would then show up to heal, set free, deliver, restore and most importantly cleanse us from all unrighteousness.

For many of you doors have been unlocked that have been jammed shut for years. God has opened you up to cleanse you and to give you the power to forget and press forward. For others sin in your life has been exposed, but we rejoice because we know that if we confess our sin, God is faithful and just to forgive us of our sins and to cleanse us from all unrighteousness.

The Lord is here right now to do the same for you right where you are if you will allow Him to work in your life.

- He saw the infirm woman. **God has seen you**.
- He called her to Him. **God is calling you to Himself today…DADDY WANTS HIS BABY GIRLS TO COME TO HIM!**
- He said to her: woman you are loosed from your infirmity. **Daddy has shown up, he is delivering, making you free from the shackles and bondages…**
- He laid hands on her. **Reach out and receive God's healing, cleansing power! Lay your hands on yourself as God releases His healing into your heart right now**
- Get this…and EXPECT THIS: Immediately she was made straight and glorified God. **Immediately you will be cleansed, made whole, delivered, set free and reconciled to God…GLORIFY HIM!**

Be Blessed! Please write to me and let me know what the Lord has done for you, or if you have further questions, feel free to email me at tbwoman@bellsouth.net.

Personal Thoughts:

CHAPTER EIGHT

5 Things Every Parent Needs To Know

You need to *Know* God & God must *Know* you. *"But as many as received Him, to them He gave the right to become children of God, to those who believe in His name."* (John 1:12) The Bible also says, *"...but rather rejoice because your names are written in heaven."* (Luke 10:20). It's not enough to know "about" God or to have heard or even acknowledge that there is a God. As a godly parent you need to KNOW that you know God the way that He said we are to enter into a relationship with Him (*Romans 10:9, 10*); *and* you must *know* that He *knows* you, by way of your name being written in His book in heaven with a full assurance that you are in correct, right-standing relationship with the Almighty. There are many people who think simply because they "believe" in God and even "pray" to God that they are in proper relationship with Him. This is not necessarily true. If you have never surrendered your life to the Lord, then you may not have the assurance that you know God properly and that He knows you intimately as one of His children. Mom, Dad, you must know God and He must know you!

You need to KNOW the Word of God. As godly parents, we must realize that we are to be "distribution centers" for our children. We should possess what they need to be the men and women that God intended them to be. This is why it is imperative that we have an intimate, working knowledge of the Word of God tucked away in our hearts, so that we are able to supply our children with godly wisdom, instruction and encouragement when they need it. *"Your word I have hidden in my heart, that I might not sin against You. I will meditate on Your precepts, and contemplate Your ways. I will delight myself in Your statutes; I will not forget Your word." Psalms 119:11; 15-16*

You must know yourself. You are exactly what your child needs to become the man or woman that God intended for them to be, but it's going to take all of who you are to help them. If you are not sure about you, or don't know yourself (the good, bad and ugly), then you will have a difficult time with parenting. We must realize that the "who" we are directly impacts and influences the "who" they are. We are not required to be perfect, have all the answers or be able to "walk on water," but we must be honest, open and real about who we are and where we are in our own developing and growing process. And we must know ourselves—our strengths, our weaknesses, our limitations and our abilities. By engaging in a constant learning program about ourselves and constantly seeking to improve the "who" we are, we will ensure happier and more secure children. The Bible says that God demands that we be open and honest about the "real" us. *"Behold, You desire truth in the inward parts..." Psalm 51:6*

We must *know* our purpose as parents. What do parents do? Well, here is a short list of our "jobs" as parents: trainer, leader, guide, coach, motivator, builder, provider, corrector, disciplinarian, and child of God. Our job is not to order, boss around, dictate to, use or abuse our children. We are not supposed to be making our children become "little" versions of ourselves...we are truly to take the purpose, destiny and gift that God has given us in the form of our child and lead him toward God's plans for his life, so that he will become the man (or woman) that God wants him to be.

We must know that we are *able* to do this. You can be the absolute best parent possible for your child. As long as we continue to learn, grow and expand…and as long as we can remain open, honest and transparent, we won't have any trouble winning the love, affection and respect of our children for the rest of our lives.

5 Things Every Parent Should Know Questionnaire

Below are some questions to ask yourself and give answers to.

- Do you know God (not just know "about" Him, but *know* Him)?
- Do you love God with all your heart, soul and mind? (Jesus said, *"He who has my commandments and keeps them, it is he who loves Me. And he who loves Me will be loved by My Father, and I will love him and manifest Myself to him."* John 14:21)
- Do you know the Word of God?
- Do you obey the Word (voice) of God in your life daily?
- Do you know yourself?
- Are you honest with yourself?
- Are you at "peace" with yourself?
- Are you growing and trying to improve yourself?
- Do you understand your purpose as a parent?
- Are you willing to train your child in the way the your child should go?

- Are you willing to ask God to tell you which way your child should go, and then go the way God shows you?
- Are you willing and ready to correct and discipline your child?
- Can you motivate, encourage and respect your child?
- Can you provide everything that your child needs materially?
- Do you have issues with or about your parents that you think may influence the way you parent your own child(ren)?
- Have you left your past behind?
- Do you know that you truly are ready to be a parent?
- Do you know that you are truly able to be a parent?
- Do you want to be a parent?
- How will you know that you have successfully raised your child/children?

Personal Thoughts:

Parenting Wisdom
From the book of Proverbs

Here are some scriptures for you to meditate on during your journey becoming a great parent.

A wise man will hear and increase learning, and a man of understanding will attain wise counsel
Proverbs 1:5

The fear of the Lord is the beginning of knowledge, but fools despise wisdom and instruction
Proverbs 1:7

He stores up sound wisdom for the upright; He is a shield to those who walk uprightly
Proverbs 2:7

Trust in the Lord with all your heart, and lean not on your own understanding; in all your ways acknowledge Him, and He shall direct your paths.
Proverbs 3:5-6

For whom the Lord loves He corrects, just as a father the son in whom he delights.
Proverbs 3:12

The curse of the Lord is on the house of the wicked, But He blesses the home of the just
Proverbs 3:33

Wisdom is the principal thing; therefore get wisdom and in all your getting, get understanding.
Proverbs 4:7

In the multitude of words sin is not lacking, but he who restrains his lips is wise.
Proverbs 10:19

He who troubles his own house will inherit the wind, and the fool will be servant to the wise of heart.
Proverbs 11:29

A wise son heeds his father's instruction, but a scoffer does not listen to rebuke.
Proverbs 13:1

He who walks with wise men will be wise, but the companion of fools will be destroyed.
Proverbs 13:20

A good man leaves an inheritance to his children's children, but the wealth of the sinner is stored up for the righteous.
Proverbs 13:22

He who spares his rod hates his son, but he who loves him disciplines him promptly (early).
Proverbs 13:24

The wise woman builds her house, but the foolish pulls it down with her hands.
Proverbs 14:1

In the fear of the Lord there is strong confidence, and His children will have a place of refuge.
Proverbs 14:26

He who is slow to wrath has great understanding, but he who is impulsive exalts folly.
Proverbs 14:29

A soft answer turns away wrath, but a harsh word stirs up anger.
Proverbs 15:1

Harsh discipline is for him who forsakes the way, and he who hates correction will die.
Proverbs 15:10

A foolish son is a grief to his father, and bitterness to her who bore him.
Proverbs 17:25

He who has knowledge spares his words, and a man of understanding is of a calm spirit.
Proverbs 17:18

Even a fool is counted wise when he holds his peace; when he shuts his lips, he is considered perceptive.
Proverbs 17:18

He who answers a matter before he hears it, it is folly and shame to him.
Proverbs 18:13

A foolish son is the ruin of his father
Proverbs 19:13

Chasten your son while there is hope, and do not set your heart on his destruction.
Proverbs 19:18

Even a child is known by his deeds, whether what he does is pure and right.
Proverbs 20:11

Train up a child in the way he should go, and when he is old he will not depart from it.
Proverbs 22:6

Foolishness is bound up in the heart of a child; the rod of correction will drive it far from him.
Proverbs 22:15

Do not withhold correction from a child, for if you beat him with a rod, he will not die. You shall beat him with a rod and deliver his soul from hell.
Proverbs 23:13-14

Listen to your father who begot you, and do not despise your mother when she is old.
Proverbs 23:22

Let your father and your mother be glad, and let her who bore you rejoice.
Proverbs 23:25

Through wisdom a house is built, and by understanding it is established; by knowledge the rooms are filled with all precious and pleasant riches.
Proverbs 24:3-4

It is not good to show partiality in judgment
Proverbs 24:23

The rod and rebuke give wisdom, but a child left to himself brings shame to his mother.
Proverbs 29:15

Correct your son and he will give you rest; yes, he will give delight to your soul.
Proverbs 29:17

She watches over the ways of her household, and does not eat the bread of idleness. Her children rise up and call her blessed; her husband also
Proverbs 31:27-28

Scriptures that mean the most to me:

Personal Thoughts:

CHAPTER NINE

The Wealthy Woman— Getting My Money Straight

Women face unique challenges that amount to different financial needs.

- Women live longer than men (an average of 7 years) so they need 20% more for retirement.
- On average, women earn 25% less than men.
- Since women tend to take time off to raise children or take care of parents, they save less than men do for retirement.
- After earning lower salaries for fewer years, women's social security benefits are about half of men's.
- Almost 1 in 4 women are broke within two months of a husband passing away.
- 53% of women are not covered by a pension compared to only 22% of men.
- A staggering 87% of the poverty stricken elderly are women.
- Three out of four women are single when they die.

- 75% of caretakers for elderly parents are women.
- Two out of three women do not participate in an employer-sponsored 401 K pension or retirement plan.
- Women are awarded child custody in 86% of divorces, and 50% of child-support payments are received only in part or not at all.
- Women are 52% of the population.
- There are over 9.1 million women-owned businesses in the U.S. representing about 38% if all businesses.
- Women-owned businesses employ 27.5 million people and generate over $3.6 trillion in sales.
- Women-owned businesses are expected to increase to 50% of all businesses in the U.S. by 2005.
- In 20 years, two-thirds of America's wealthy will be female.
- Women are starting businesses at a rate twice that of men, with a lower failure rate.
- Women-owned firms are found in all industries.

God's Thoughts on Finances
For the Wealthy Woman

The Lord is very clear to us that He wants and enjoys the prosperity of His daughters. Here are just a few scriptures to prove that:

Let them shout for joy and be glad, who favor my righteous cause; and let them say continually, Let the Lord be magnified, who has pleasure in the prosperity of His servant. Psalm 35:27
(The Hebrew word translated "prosperity" in the above verse is shalom, which literally means, "completeness, soundness, welfare and peace" in every area of your existence.)

Do not fear, little flock, for it is your Father's good pleasure
to give you the kingdom.
Luke 13:32
(This embraces it all because here God is telling us that
whatever the kingdom has to offer, He wants you to have it.
Keep in mind, there is no sickness in the kingdom of heaven.
There is no disease, infirmity, poverty, lack, oppression,
schism, or division there either.)

But this I say: He who sows sparingly will also reap
sparingly, and he who sows bountifully will also reap
bountifully. So let each one give as he purposes in his heart,
not grudgingly or of necessity; for God loves a cheerful
giver. And God is able to make all grace abound toward
you, that you, always having all sufficiency in all things,
may have an abundance for every good work.
2 Corinthians 9:6-8

The rich rules over the poor, and the borrower is servant to
the lender.
Proverbs 22:7

He who has a slack hand becomes poor, but the hand of the
diligent makes rich.
Proverbs 10:4

A good man leaves an inheritance to his children's children,
but the wealth of the sinner is stored up for the righteous.
Proverbs 13:33

But if anyone does not provide for his own, and especially
for those of his household, he has denied the faith, and is
worse than an unbeliever.
1 Timothy 5:8

We must remember, money does not and can not buy happiness…money simply creates ability. We need to talk about our expectations instead of our experiences with money and we definitely need to focus and discuss our future and not our past.

The past is used for historical reference only. It is not a determinant of where you are going or what is in store for you!

So what exactly is on God's mind for the wealthy woman? Well, if we obey Him and keep all of His commandments, then we can expect:

1. Blessings will be upon us.
2. Blessings will overtake us.
3. Blessings in the city.
4. Blessings in the country.
5. Blessings in the fruit of our body (offspring).
6. Blessings in the produce of our ground (our places of employment).
7. Increase in every area of our lives.
8. Blessings when we come in.
9. Blessings when we go out.
10. Our enemies will be defeated before our faces; they will flee before us seven ways.
11. Command of blessing in our storehouses (bank accounts).
12. Command of blessing in all that we set our hand.
13. Blessings in the land (or place) that the Lord has given to you (your sphere of influence in this world).
14. Establishment as a holy people unto the Lord.
15. All of the people of the earth shall SEE that you are called.
16. The Lord will grant us plenty of goods.

17. The Lord will open to us his good treasure.
18. We will lend to many, but we will not have to borrow.
19. The Lord will make us the head.
20. We will be above only.

*Praying the Word of God for
Today's Wealthy Woman*

Take your favorite mini-prayers from the group listed and pray them over yourself and your finances daily.

I thank you Father, that You supply all of my needs according to Your riches in glory in Christ Jesus.
Philippians 4:19

Father, I thank You that because I seek first Your kingdom and Your righteousness, all of these natural things are added to me.
Matthew 6:33

Father, I believe that Your divine power has granted to me everything pertaining to life and godliness through the true knowledge of You through Your word. I have everything I need concerning life.
2 Peter 1:3

I thank You, Father, that You, the God of peace, equip and supply me with every good thing to do Your will.
Hebrews 13:20, 21

The Lord is my Shepherd, and I shall not lack for any good thing in my life.
Psalm 23:1

Father, I thank You that because I walk uprightly before You, You don't withhold from me any good thing.
Psalm 84:11

Lord, I thank You that because I keep Your Word in my mouth and meditate on it day and night, making sure that I do all that is written in it, I make my way prosperous, and I always have success.
Joshua 1:8

Because I am willing and obedient, I eat the best of the land.
Isaiah 1:19

Because I delight in the law of the Lord, and in His law I meditate day and night, I'm like a tree firmly planted by streams of water, which yields its fruit in its season, and its leaf does not wither; and in whatever I do, I prosper.
Psalm 1:2,3

I thank You Father, that because I bring the whole tithe into the storehouse, You throw open the floodgates of heaven and You pour out so much blessing upon me that I don't have enough room for it.
Malachi 3:10

Lord You said in Your word that although our Lord Jesus Christ was rich, yet for our sakes He became poor, that we through His poverty, might become rich. Father, I thank You right now that those riches are manifested in my life in Jesus' name.
2 Corinthians 8:9

The blessing of the Lord makes me rich, and He adds no sorrow to it.
Proverbs 10:22

Father, I thank You that you give me the treasures of darkness and the hidden wealth of secret places in order that I may know that it is You, the Lord, the God of Israel, who calls me by my name.
Isaiah 45:3

Financial Biblical Wisdom for the Wealthy Woman

Use the scriptures listed below to get an understanding of what God expects of Wealthy Women.

A wise woman will hear and increase learning, and a woman of understanding will attain (acquire) wise counsel.
Proverbs 1:5

The fear of the Lord is the beginning of knowledge, but fools despise wisdom and instruction.
Proverbs 1:7

So are the ways of everyone who is greedy for gain; it takes away the life of its owners.
Proverbs 1:19

So that you incline you ear to wisdom and apply your heart to understanding; for the Lord gives wisdom; from His mouth come knowledge and understanding; He stores up sound wisdom for the upright
Proverbs 2:2, 6-7

When wisdom enters your heart, and knowledge is pleasant to your soul, discretion will preserve you; understanding will keep you
Proverbs 2:10-11

Trust in the Lord with all your heart, and lean not on your own understanding. In all your ways acknowledge Him and He shall direct your paths.
Proverbs 3:5-6

Honor the Lord with your possessions and with the first-fruits of all your increase; so your barns will be filled with plenty, and your vats will overflow with new wine.
Proverbs 3:9-10

Wisdom is the principal thing; therefore get wisdom, and in all your getting, get understanding. Proverbs 4:7

Go to the ant, you sluggard! Consider her ways and be wise, which having no captain, overseer or ruler, provides her supplies in the summer, and gathers her food in the harvest.
Proverbs 6:6-8

I love those who love me, and those who seek me diligently will find me. Riches and honor are with me, enduring riches and righteousness. My fruit is better than gold, yes, than fine gold, and my revenue than choice silver. That I may cause those who love me to inherit wealth, that I may fill their treasuries.
Proverbs 17, 18, 19; 21

He who has a slack hand becomes poor, but the hand of the diligent makes rich.
Proverbs 10:4

He who gathers in summer is a wise daughter; he who sleeps in harvest is a daughter who causes shame.
Proverbs 10:5

The blessing of the Lord makes one rich, and He adds no sorrow with it.
Proverbs 10:22

The integrity of the upright will guide them, but the perversity of the unfaithful will destroy them.
Proverbs 11:3

Where there is no counsel, the people fall; but in the multitude of counselors there is safety.
Proverbs 11:14

A gracious woman retains honor, but ruthless men retain riches.
Proverbs 11:16

The generous soul will be made rich, and he who waters will also be watered himself.
Proverbs 11:25

The hand of the diligent will rule, but the lazy man will be put to forced labor.
Proverbs 12:24

The soul of a lazy woman desires, and has nothing; but the soul of the diligent shall be made rich.
Proverbs 13:4

Wealth gained by dishonesty will be diminished, but he who gathers by labor will increase.
Proverbs 13:11

Poverty and shame will come to her who disdains correction, but she who regards rebuke will be honored.
Proverbs 13:18

A good woman leaves an inheritance to her children's
children, but the wealth of the sinner is stored up for the
righteous.
Proverbs 13:22

The preparations of the heart belong to woman, but the
answer of the tongue is from the Lord.
Proverbs 16:1

Commit your works to the Lord, and your thoughts will be
established.
Proverbs 16:3

When a woman's ways please the Lord, He makes even her
enemies to be at peace with her.
Proverbs 16:7

A woman's heart plans her way, but the Lord directs her
steps.
Proverbs 16:9

How much better to get wisdom than gold! And to get
understanding is to be chosen rather than silver.
Proverbs 16:16

Wealth makes many friends, but the poor is separated from
her friend.
Proverbs 19:4

Luxury is not fitting for a fool, much less for a servant to
rule over princes.
Proverbs 19:10

Laziness casts one into a deep sleep, and an idle person will
suffer hunger.
Proverbs 19:15

He who has pity on the poor lends to the Lord, and He will pay back what he has given.
Proverbs 19:17

Do not love sleep, lest you come to poverty; open your eyes and you will be satisfied with bread.
Proverbs 20:13

Plans are established by counsel; by wise counsel wage war.
Proverbs 20:18

The plans of the diligent lead surely to plenty, but those of everyone who is hasty, surely to poverty.
Proverbs 21:5

Getting treasures by a lying tongue is the fleeting fantasy of those who seek death.
Proverbs 21:6

She who loves pleasure will be a poor woman, she who loves wine and oil will not be rich.
Proverbs 21:17

The rich rules over the poor, and the borrower is servant to the lender.
Proverbs 22:7

She who has a generous eye will be blessed, for she gives of her bread to the poor.
Proverbs 22:9

Do not overwork to be rich; because of your own understanding, cease.
Proverbs 23:4

I went by the field of the lazy woman, and by the vineyard of the woman devoid of understanding; and there it was, all overgrown with thorns; its surface was covered with nettles; its stone wall was broken down, when I saw it, I considered it well; I looked on it and received instruction; a little sleep, a little slumber, a little folding of the hands to rest; so shall your poverty come like a prowler, and your need like an armed man.
Proverbs 24:30-34

Whoever has no rule over her own spirit, is like a city broken down, without walls.
Proverbs 25:28

Be diligent to know the state of your flocks, and attend to your herds; for riches are not forever, nor does a crown endure to all generations.
Proverbs 27:23-24

Better is the poor who walks in her integrity than one perverse in her ways, though she be rich.
Proverbs 28:6

A faithful man will abound with blessings, but he who hastens to be rich will not go unpunished.
Proverbs 28:20

A man with an evil eye hastens after riches, and does not consider that poverty will come upon him.
Proverbs 28:2

My favorite scriptures:

Selah...Pause, Think and TAKE ACTION
Your Financial Goals

Financial goals are measurable items that you can begin to tackle today.

Biblical Guidelines for Financial Goal Setting

1. Get God's Thoughts About You. The Wealthy Woman learns His plan for your financial future. *"Thus says the Lord your Redeemer, the Holy One of Israel: I am the Lord your God, Who teaches you to profit, Who leads you by the way you should go." Isaiah 48:17*

2. Write down your top four goals. It helps to make them realistic and easy. *"Write the vision and make it plain..." Habakkuk 2:2*

3. Remember, goals must be specific, measurable and provable. For example, what not to do: "I want to be wealthy in the year 2001." What is more realistic is to say, "My goal is to put aside X% of my income in a retirement account for the next year." *"His heart is established; he will not be afraid, until he sees his desire upon his enemies." Psalm 112:8*

4. Start Today, Right Now! Take immediate action within 48 hours. Make a phone call or look up some information you need—your goal will feel more realistic. *"But be doers of the word and not hearers only, deceiving yourselves." James 1:22*

5. Put a written copy of your goals where you can see them everyday. *"...make it plain on tablets, that he may run who reads it." Habakkuk 2:2*

6. Develop goals that fit with God's plan for your life. *"...for it is the Father's good pleasure to give you the kingdom." Luke 13:32*

7.   Review your goals at least every 12 months. At a minimum review your goals once a year at a time you designate. This will help to keep you on track or refocus your efforts. *"My son, give attention to my words...do not let them depart from your eyes; keep them in the midst of your heart."* Proverbs 4:20 - 21

GOAL	DATE

Your financial plan should center around "doable" action goals. For example the first step in your financial plan could be to have the goal of creating an emergency fund equaling X number of month's pay. Your action step is to begin saving by bringing lunches to work; reduce impulse buying; put aside money in a savings or money market account, etc. Remember, remember, remember, your "plan" should come from the "Most High Planner, God Himself!" It is much simpler to execute a "plan" that God has given to you!

Remember:

"A man's heart plans his way, but the Lord directs his steps."
Proverbs 16:9

"…I am the Lord your God Who teaches you to profit, Who leads you by the way you should go."
Isaiah 48:17

"The fear of the Lord is the beginning of knowledge, but fools despise wisdom and instruction."
Proverbs 1:7

Signs of Trouble, Financial Checklist

✓ You pay only the minimum on your credit cards.
✓ You've been denied credit.
✓ You pay half your bills one month and half the next.
✓ You can't save, even small amounts.
✓ You often get calls from creditors or collectors about unpaid bills.
✓ You frequently bounce checks.
✓ You have to work a part-time job or work overtime to make ends meet.
✓ You put off going to the doctor because you can't afford the visit.
✓ You post date checks.
✓ You constantly worry about money.
✓ You hide credit card bills and/or receipts from your spouse.

✓ You have trouble making rent or house payments on time.
✓ You pay off one charge card with another charge card.
✓ You live paycheck to paycheck.
✓ You tap your savings to pay for day-to-day expenses.
✓ You've consolidated your debt, but continue to use credit cards.
✓ You take cash advances to pay daily living expenses.
✓ You sign up for other cards because you've hit the limit on current cards.
✓ You find yourself always out of cash.

Answering "yes" to just one of these statements could mean you're in trouble or heading for trouble.

What to do Immediately if You are in Trouble:

1. Add up your debt to get a realistic picture of your financial situation.
2. Stop charging! Put away your cards.
3. Read your past few statements to see how you've been spending your money. Use the information to make a monthly budget and stick with it.
4. Look for areas where you can cut back spending, and use that money to reduce your debt. Eat out less. Cancel your cable. Take the bus. Avoid late fees by paying your bills on time. Do whatever it takes to stop the bleeding!
5. Talk to your lenders. You should make the first call to your lenders. Don't wait until the creditor figures out you have a problem to sort out your finances. Lenders will be much more flexible if you call them first.
6. Most lenders will help you rearrange your debt payments because it's in their best interest for you to

get back on your feet financially. Lenders may extend your payment period, help you consolidate your debt or refinance your debt.

7. Get a copy of your credit report. Credit card issuers use one or more of the three biggest bureaus to research credit history. Call each one to find out what's in your credit file. Some of the bureaus may charge a small fee, but note that you're entitled to a free copy if you're turned down for credit.

Credit Bureaus
- Equifax (800) 685-1111; www.equifax.com
- Experian (888) 397-3742; www.experian.com
- Trans Union (800) 916-8800; www.transunion.com

PROFESSIONAL CREDIT COUNSELING
- Consumer Credit Counseling Service (800) 388-2227; www.nfcc.org
- Myvesta (800) 680-3328; www.myvesta.com

Bankruptcy should be a LAST resort!
Consider the consequences before filling for bankruptcy.
1. You'll have trouble getting any type of credit for at least the next 10 years.
2. If you do get credit, you'll have to pay added finance charges or put up more collateral.
3. Explore all of your options before seeking bankruptcy.

Now it's time to make the time to list all of our financial obligations to get a clear and concise picture of where we are financially.

Personal Debt Worksheet

List all of your short and long-term debt obligations,
including creditor, type of loan, interest rate,
monthly payment and balance for each.

Creditor	Type of Credit	Interest Rate	Monthly Payment	Balance
Total:				

Bank Reconciliation
Tips, Pointers, Suggestions

TIP! You should reconcile your checking account each month.

Before you start to reconcile your monthly bank statement, check your own figures. Begin with the balance shown in your checkbook at the end of the previous month. To this balance, add the total cash deposited during the month and subtract the total cash disbursements.

After checking your figures, the result should agree with your checkbook balance at the end of the month. If the result does not agree, you may have made an error in recording a check or deposit. You can find the error by doing the following:

1. Adding the amounts on your check stubs and comparing that total with the total in the "amount of check" column in your check disbursements journal. If the totals do not agree, check the individual amounts to see if an error was made in your check stub record or in the related entry in your check disbursements journal.
2. Adding the deposit amounts in your checkbook. Compare that total with the monthly total in your cash receipt book, if you have one. If the totals do not agree, check the individual amounts to find any errors.

If your checkbook and journal entries still disagree, then refigure the running balance in your checkbook to make sure additions and subtractions are correct.

To reconcile your account, follow these steps:

1. Compare the deposits listed on the bank statement with the deposits shown in your checkbook. Note all differences in the dollar amounts.
2. Compare each cancelled check, including both check number and dollar amount, with the entry in your checkbook. Note all differences in the dollar amounts. Mark the check number in the checkbook as having cleared the bank. After accounting for all checks returned by the bank, those not marked in your checkbook are your outstanding checks.
3. Prepare a bank reconciliation.
4. Update your checkbook and journals for items shown on the reconciliation as not recorded (such as service charges) or recorded incorrectly.

At this point the adjusted bank statement balance should equal your adjusted checkbook balance. If you still have differences, check the previous steps to find errors.
Source: www.irs.ustreas.gov

Personal Thoughts:

CHAPTER TEN

A Real Career Woman—
CEO Of Your Life

First, let's take a look at the current state of affairs in today's workplace. I have two words for you: consolidation and downsizing.

Consolidation is *the unification of two or more corporations by the dissolution of existing ones and creation of a single new corporation.* To consolidate means *to join together into one whole unit; to make firm or secure; strengthen.*

Companies are absorbing one another, creating huge conglomerates. They are removing duplication in jobs, restructuring management to give a very few people incredible power and influence over vast numbers, streamlining efficiency.

What does this mean for those of us competing in this environment? Well, it leaves us vulnerable at best, and downright scared at the very least!

When "bosses" making incredible six and seven-figure salaries wind up unemployed within a matter of days, you'd better start looking around!

To compete simply means *to strive consciously or unconsciously for an objective.* You have an objective in mind…and you go after it. BUT the key in competing is what you believe. Your beliefs fuel you or discourage you. Your beliefs dictate your actions. The problem in the workplace for blacks is not necessarily "the game." The problem is what we believe about the game.

If We Believe:
- The playing field is level
- All participants know all of the rules
- There is equal access to all the tools of the game
- Fair and equitable judgment awaits all competitors
- All are judged equally

If we believe these statements, we're sunk! These are all fallacies—every one of them!

These are the internal beliefs that my husband and I enter into the game with:
1. I'm always going to win.
2. My competition (within my company/or outside my company) is as good or better than I am.
3. I'm always going to remain true to myself, my personal standards of morality and excellence.
4. My bark must always be louder, faster, harder and better than my opponent's.

John D. Rockerfeller said, "The world owes no one a living but it owes everyone an opportunity to make a living."

I figure, the world doesn't even owe me the opportunity…I intend to make my way based on what my Heavenly Father has said.

Let me give you some good news—there is a new thing going on! Some folks I call *the movers and the thinkers* of this next millennium are preaching our deliverance.

The reality is that walking down this path of consolidation, downsizing, and restructuring is going get us unemployed.

We can no longer afford to have our personal long-term interests be the same as our employer's, because friend, these companies are not considering us when decisions are being made.

Don't take it personally, it's not about black people or you as an individual, it's about cold hard cash. It's about power, greed and the American way of business. I don't take it personally. I don't get mad…I get smart!

3 Secrets to our Success: We Must

- BE _PROACTIVE_ INSTEAD OF _REACTIVE!_
- WE MUST BE _VICTORS_, NOT _VICTIMS!_
- WE MUST LIVE BY _CHOICE_, NOT BY _CHANCE!_

It's been said that the happiest people in life hold themselves <u>fully accountable</u> for their own actions and waste no time in blame-fixing or excuse-making. They put up or shut up!

A true sign of maturity is that you realize and act according to the fact that your decisions cause your rewards and your consequences!

CEO of out Daily Lives

Now, for the new paradigm...it's called being the *CEO of our daily lives.*

Being CEO of our daily lives means *to think of ourselves as a one-person company that provides services to other companies.*

We must act self-employed from now on—moving from a *job-oriented* mindset to a *skill-oriented* mindset.

I believe the hottest commodity of the next millennium is going to be people: you and me. It's going to be the gifts, talents, thoughts, concepts, execution style, integrity and morality that we have to offer. We will be our own service company with a single employee that puts its services to work for larger companies.

As CEO of our lives, we should no longer think of ourselves as someone's employee. Employees come and go; they're hired and fired based on the company's needs, desires or decisions.

But as micro, one-person businesses now you're on a mission. This is the mindset we must possess to be victors in this new millennium.

We must
- Develop a personal training department within our one-person company. We must ensure that we have the skills and information that we'll need to meet the demands of the changing workplace. We must keep updating our skills!

- Dissolve our current way of viewing and thinking about our careers. We must reinvent ourselves to meet changing demands.

The idea is that you take a long, hard, tough look at yourself and you begin with asking the questions:
1. How vulnerable am I?
2. What can I do about my vulnerability?
3. What trends must I watch?
4. What knowledge do I lack?
5. What information must I gain?

Every company worth its salt invests time and money into research and development. It's time we did some research and development for ourselves. Go back to school if necessary. Hone up our skills, update our talents. Make sure we are marketable today!

I believe that we need to change our core thinking about what we call skills and talents. The reality is that anything can be refined into a skill or talent and sold in the marketplace.

Talking, reading, laughing, thinking can be developed into marketable skills.

It's self-assessment time and it's also choice-making time.

This new workplace will see us as CEOs providing services to larger companies. This means if your "service" is being the best organizer there is, you can organize for any number of industries—banking, media, technology—you name it. We should be thinking as single-person companies that can provide our wares for any number of companies.

There's no more "go to school to study X career. Graduate, get job at X company doing X career, retire in thirty years and get the gold watch." That's obsolete. There may not be a company tomorrow…what will you do then? We must be prepared!

We must
- Take personal inventory/stock
- Be honest with ourselves
- Hone up on our key gifts/talents
- Have a personal/company mission statement
- Keep updated/educated about our fields
- Expect the unexpected, don't be caught unaware/sleeping

I know we are going to need much training. I am committed to the training process with as many people as I can reach. We are going to need leaders and thinkers that can take us through these processes and give us clear, easy to understand principles to apply in our daily lives today. I'm more than willing to help in any way that I can.

I'd like to end these thoughts with the dream of all dreams. It comes from a statement from James Olmos the actor.

James said, "Chase your passion not your pension." I love that! What I am doing with Today's Black Woman isn't my career, my job, my work…it's who I am, what I was designed by God to do. I love it! I don't turn it off at night or turn it on in the morning. I don't drag myself into the office—I live, sleep, eat, think and create Today's Black Woman always!

I'm trying every way I can to inspire black folk to stop chasing after this artificial dream. We have allowed the world to dictate to us what our success is. Success for you is not the same as success for me. If we buy into the big house, the BMW and the big, fat paycheck and that's it—we've lost before we've started. I read the statement "If you chase money, it may catch you—and if it catches you, you'll forever be its slave."

Never work for money; focus in on that thing that you'd do even if you were paid nothing beyond food and the basics. Do it because it's your life!

8 Ways To Become Personally and Professionally Empowered

1. ***Start from where you are and take one step at a time.*** Where you are right now is the perfect place to begin going to the next level! Begin with your present perceptions, attitudes, "issues" and strengths, then move...one step at a time.
2. ***Don't be resistant to change.*** We resist when we need to delve into the unknown. Remember that *change* and *time* are your friends, not your enemies. Embrace change, welcome change, get excited...you'll never be the same again.
3. ***Recognize that where you are and what you are experiencing right now can be used for your growth and development.*** Midnight comes, but there is always a new morning just around the corner. Trials, circumstances, negativity and hard times can be used as the lemons that we eventually turn into lemonade in our lives. Want to know the secret of enduring through the storms and turbulence? Let patience have its perfect

work. When you learn the art of focusing in on something else *in the meantime* then at the end of your hard times, you will find yourself perfect and complete lacking nothing.

4. *Leave your past behind.* Your past is for *historical reference* only. It is no indication of your future. Leave it behind, kiss it good-bye—it has no bearing on where we're headed.

5. *Finish your unfinished business.* Most of us have *unfinished business*—unresolved issues—failed marriages, broken relationships, owed money, whatever. Here are four things you can do *today* to press forward: *Recognize* the part you played in the issue. *Take responsibility* for your part. *Apologize*, if necessary, for the role you played and most importantly: *MOVE ON!* Get over it; it's history...drop it!

6. *Be proactive instead of reactive.* Proactively make strides past your fears, failures and obstacles of life. Fulfill your *God-given* purpose.

7. *Become a victor instead of a victim.* We are victorious first in our minds. Think positively and know beyond a shadow of a doubt you are destined for a glorious future.

8. *Live by choice, not by chance. Movers* and *thinkers* in this new century understand this basic personal and professional survival key: *Life is a series of choices that I make!* Choose your life...and to live a life that is full, happy and complete. Invest in you, take time for living with your spouse, family and friends...maximize your life!

CHAPTER ELEVEN

Empowering Affirmations— 31 Days to a New You

Take a moment to read each affirmation daily.
Then throughout your day ponder,
think about and meditate the affirmation.
Each one is based on the Word of God
and will bring "God's thinking" and "God's life"
into your life. Be blessed!

1. I can do all things through Christ who strengthens me!
2. Mercy and goodness follow me all the days of my life!
3. I am blessed—empowered to prosper!
4. Everything that I touch turns to gold…the work of my hands is blessed!
5. All of my needs are met according to God's riches in glory through Christ!
6. I believe that everything that the Lord has spoken to me for my life will be accomplished!
7. My mind is renewed and I am transformed into the woman God wants me to be!
8. Peace…*nothing missing and nothing broken*…permeates and rules in my life and heart!
9. Stress, sickness, *dis*-ease, worry and pain must go out of my life today!

10. The Lord is good to me and His mercy endures in my life forever!
11. God loves me…even me…especially me…all the days of my life!
12. I am above in all circumstances in my life…above only and never beneath!
13. I seek first God's ways of doing things and then everything else is added to me!
14. I seek after and find God's wisdom every day of my life and I prosper through it!
15. I don't allow anger, strife or upset to rule on the inside of me!
16. I keep my temper in check!
17. I don't use my mouth as a garbage can…I speak only what is uplifting to the hearer!
18. I don't allow my heart to be a garbage can…I guard my heart hourly!
19. I am more than a conqueror through Christ!
20. I choose God above all and every one else!
21. I no longer have to live my life under the curse of poverty or ruin in any area of my life!
22. I lay aside, strip off, and throw off any weights, issues or people who try to stop me from running my race!
23. I will accomplish all of my heart's desires in my lifetime!
24. I am satisfied with long, abundant life in Christ!
25. My body is well, healed and whole!
26. I am forgiven by the blood and work of Jesus Christ!
27. I have eternal life with God through Jesus Christ!
28. I am free from guilt and condemnation!
29. I walk by faith in what God's word says, not by my natural sight!
30. The Lord leads me in the way that I should go and teaches me how to profit!

31. I am a beautiful woman from the inside out…working on my inner beauty, a peaceable, quite spirit!

31 DAYS TO A NEW YOU
Use this calendar to check the days off

1	2	3	4	5	6	7
8	9	10	11	12	13	14
15	16	17	18	19	20	21
22	23	24	25	26	27	28
29	30	31				

A Personal Devotion Just For You

"For My thoughts are not your thoughts, nor are your ways My ways, says the Lord. For as the heavens are higher than the earth, so are My ways higher than your ways, and My thoughts than your thoughts."
Isaiah 55:9-10

Happy New Life! Are you hopeful, expectant, and ready to take on your life with a vengeance? We think we have our lives all figured out, don't we? Just a few more moves to secure that next promotion. A few more payments to pay off that debt. Just meet Mr. Right and I'll be married and my life will be better. Just lose a few more pounds and I'll look and feel better, and the list goes on and on.

We've all made those infamous "New Year's Resolutions," only to be ashamed, disgusted and embarrassed a few weeks later, when we've failed to keep a single one. So, what's a woman to do you ask? I'll tell you what—we all need to re-acquaint ourselves with one simple and profound truth: We've got Someone on our side that has a much better plan for our lives!

"For My thoughts are not your thoughts." That financial plan you're about to execute, albeit good, is not God's thoughts for your finances. His are higher and greater. That plan to go back to school to get the degree to get the better job, although it's to be commended, it is not necessarily what God's thinking of for your life. He's always thinking something higher, better and more excellent for you. Does this mean we chuck all of our ideas, thoughts, plans and reasoning, and live life without direction? God forbid! It simply means that we all should and could come up higher to where God's perspective is, to where God's

thoughts are, to where we can see clearer and fresher from God's position, power and authority.

I don't know about you, but this excites me because it means that my best plan is where God begins. My best strategy for my life and the lives of my children is exactly where God picks up and begins the play-by-play. Not only is He thinking higher, better more excellent thoughts, the way He goes about instructing me to implement His plan for my life is greater. See, all I have to do is go to God, get His higher and more excellent plan and then begin implementing the plan that He gives me. This is so much different from what we do on a daily basis. We think about how something should be done, then begin trying to make it happen on our own and then down the road when things get crazy we ask God to bless the mess we've made! This is exactly why He tells us, look guys, I'm not going to do it the way you think—My ways and thoughts are always going to be higher.

"So are My ways higher than your ways." Higher ways—instead of four moves up the corporate ladder, it's one move. Instead of thirty-nine more payments to pay off that debt, it's two, or better still, it's cancelled. Instead of going back to school to better your job, it's starting your own God-appointed and anointed business. Higher ways mean efficient movement, upward mobility and manifested results that are sure and undoubtedly GOD!

God didn't say not to have thoughts or ways of getting where you want to go. In fact the Bible is full of wisdom that says planning and choosing God's ways equal a greater life. But when we feel our way is the only way or that our thoughts are the only thoughts, we truly get messed up.

I know you want to save your marriage but you think it can't work. Just remember, "My thoughts aren't your thoughts…and My ways are higher than your ways," says the Lord. I know you might think all hope is gone or that you'll be stuck in life where you are right now…wrong! "For as the heavens are higher than the earth, so are My ways higher than your ways." Heaven's plan is higher than what's going on here in the earth. Heaven's mentality is one of wealth, riches, peace, success and harmony. Heaven is far above debilitating sickness, eviction notices, low self-esteem or divorce.

Our thoughts for our lives at their best don't equal the thoughts, ways, plans and strategies that God has for us.

"For I know the thoughts that I think toward you, says the Lord, thoughts of peace and not of evil, to give you a future and a hope. Then you will call upon Me and go and pray to Me and I will listen to you. And you will seek Me and find Me, when you search for Me with all your heart. I will be found by you, says the Lord, and I will bring you back from your captivity…"
Jeremiah 29:11-14a

God says He knows what He's thinking about you. Peace and not evil, to give you a hope and a future. Hope, a future, plans, purpose, fulfillment, happiness in life—in a nutshell, life like God has it. How exciting! All we have to do is call on Him, pray to Him, get inside His head and find out what His plan is for our lives. He's already promised to listen and to be found by us if we will seek Him with all our hearts.

Are you ready to be brought back from captivity? Then let's start calling upon God. Let's start humbling ourselves, realizing that our best is still not going to ultimately cut it and let's start seeking our God, praying to our God and searching for our God. He's thinking peaceful thoughts about you right now. He's thinking about your future, your success, your overcoming, your happiness, your prosperity right now. Can't your see His face lit with joy, waiting with His arms open...

Let's start from this day forward searching for the one true and living God. And He has already promised that if we truly seek Him with our whole heart... "I will be found by you, says the Lord!"

Find Him today!

Empowerment Action Plan:

List one important plan, goal or thought you have for your life this month:

_____

_____

 List two key things that you can do starting today to make this happen:

_____

_____

_____

Private Thoughts:

A Personal Devotion Just For You

"Trust in the Lord with all your heart..."
Proverbs 3:5

How can you trust someone you do not know or aren't in a real relationship with? It's impossible, isn't it? Trust can't be developed, built and flow between two people until there has been ample time and relationship and experience between the individuals.

When we've shared our hearts, our thoughts; when we've watched one another's integrity and honesty, when we've gone down the road long enough to know that we can really believe in one another, then trust begins to develop, grow and flourish in our key relationships.

Let's be honest—in this day and age, we really don't trust people. People have disappointed us, let us down, used and abused us. We separate ourselves from the intimacy of relationship because we are afraid of being let down and hurt. I believe that it's no accident that humans have grown to distrust and shun one another. I believe we have been led down this path, very methodically, so that we would not give trust easily to one another and subsequently wouldn't give trust to our heavenly Father.

You see, God needs, wants, and demands our trust in Him. It's the foundation of our faith. We must know beyond a shadow of a doubt that God will never leave us hanging; He'll never betray us; He'll always be on our side. Trust is reliance, assurance; it's confidence that what was said is true and will be done by the individual. I don't have to wonder whether or not my husband will bring home a paycheck and take care of me and the kids, because I trust that Tony will do right by us. The trust that I have developed with my husband has come through many circumstances, trials and situations in which he's proven time and time again, he's a man who can be trusted to do what he says he's going to do. That brings great relief and joy to me, because I can count on him if I can't count on any one else!

How much more my heavenly Father! You see, over the years of being in relationship with my Lord, He's proven time and time and time again to me that I can trust Him. I can trust His guidance in business affairs as well as matters of the heart. I can trust Him to lead me through difficult times and tough decisions as well as bring me to blessings and peace and joy unspeakable. I've taken the time to get to know Him. To know God means to know not only what He has said, but to know His ways.

Trust in the Lord. Four, simple, life-changing words. If you will commit in your heart right now to begin to develop your own unique, personal relationship with the Lord, you too can trust Him. The thing about God is that we must do things His way. You see, in relationships, any relationship, the two parties involved set the boundaries and "rules" if you will for the relationship. Within these carefully constructed boundaries the two parties are free to enjoy one another in endless hours of bliss as long as neither party violates the rules.

Well, God has already given the guidelines for relationship with Him. We must come through the work of the cross that Jesus Christ, His Son, already accomplished for us. Far too many of us are trying to sidestep the relationship rules God has already spoken to try to enter into a relationship with God that He cannot engage in, because we've not followed His simple basic instruction.

We must "confess with our mouth the Lord Jesus and believe in our heart that God has raised Him from the dead, and then we will be saved (Romans 10:9)." I'm not talking about mouthing some simple words. I'm talking about the real acknowledgement that we are in need of a Savior, because in ourselves we do not have any way of accessing a Holy and Just God. My righteousness doesn't cut it with God, I knew I needed help, I knew I needed God and I gladly received Jesus' work for me to gain access to Father God! Now, all who will believe and receive Jesus' work into their lives, they will be free to enter into relationship with Daddy God. If we want to be able to trust God, then we have to first begin by believing His instruction, following His instruction and doing what He has said we must do.

After approaching God and engaging in relationship with Him, He immediately begins to prove His authenticity and He immediately begins to build our belief in Him so that we can know that we can trust Him. Just sit back, and watch and see if God isn't exactly who He's said He is, and see if He won't do exactly what He said He would do for you, today.

Trust God!

Empowerment Action Plan:

Do I trust God across the board in every area of my life?
_____yes   _____no

In what area do I need to trust God more?

_____

_____

Have I entered into relationship with God the correct way, through His Son Jesus Christ?

_____yes   _____no

(Check if you really mean it!)

_____I decide today to begin building a better relationship with the Lord in which I will learn to trust Him in every area of my life.

Today's
date:_____

Private Thoughts:

A Personal Devotion Just For You

An Overcoming Overcomer

"Yet in all these things we are more than conquerors through Him who loved us. For I am persuaded that neither death nor life, nor angels nor principalities nor powers, nor things present nor things to come, nor height nor depth, nor any other created thing shall be able to separate us from the love of God which is in Christ Jesus our Lord."
Romans 8:37-39

You are awesome! You're incredible! Created in the Master's image—God don't make NO junk! It's true. You are fearfully and wonderfully crafted inside and out. You are lovingly built—complete with hopes, dreams, desires and visions.

You know, don't let situations, circumstances, people, places or things rob you or get you down. REMEMBER: "We can do all things through Christ which strengthens us!"

Overcomers are born—overcomers do nothing except overcome! Race can't defeat you, rape, discouragement, poverty, sickness or hell itself can't win against you! Guess what? The only weapon strong enough to defeat you…is you!

Live life always relying on "He that is in you is greater than he (circumstances, places, things and people) that are in the world!"

You are an Overcoming Overcomer—and don't ever forget it!!!

Use Affirmation #1 from 31 Days to a New You today. It says, " I can do all things through Christ who strengthens me!"

Empowerment Action Plan:

1. List some things that you're currently facing now that are holding you back from overcoming. (e.g. stress, bad attitude, wrong thinking, low self-esteem)
   A.

   B.

   C.

2. Refocus through the eyes of an Overcomer and list two action steps you intend to do today to press forward. (e.g. change my attitude on purpose, budget, spend time building myself)
   A.

   B.

Private Thoughts:

A Personal Devotion Just For You

FIRE!

Fire means zeal; brilliancy, set ablaze; to inspire, "Then you call on the name of your gods, and I will call on the name of the Lord; and the God who answers by fire, He is God..." 1Kings 18:24

Burning, intense, consuming—all words that could be used when describing fire. These words can also be used to describe something deep within you. Fire—a stirring, a yearning, a longing—a passion for life, for family, your spouse, your mate, friends, or career. No matter what, sisters, please do not loose your fire and passion for your life!

Rekindle—put another log on the fire. Go back to the beginning, those first feelings, your first love. Is it poetry? Crafting? Sewing? Writing? Your man? Your children? Your love of walking by the seashore, or running through open fields? Go back to the core of what drives and motivates you—today. Go back to those first feelings—first love. First love is where passion is! First love is where fire is! First love is where you'll find the Lord waiting for you (where you left Him).

Stir up the smoldering ashes, some kindling wood is still left to burn. I know the marriage may seem bad, stale, used, abused and dead; I know the job feels like it's over; I know your kids are taxing your last nerves, I know you feel depressed, oppressed, kept down or caged in...but some ashes may still be flickering, no matter how small. Re-ignite your passion, girl, and it will take you to the next level.

You will find the next level for your family, the next level in your relationships, the next level on your job, with your parents, for your life.

Use Affirmation #6 from 31 Days to a New You today. It says, "I believe that everything that the Lord has spoken to me for my life will be accomplished!"

Empowerment Action Plan:

1. I am cold, wet, without passion and without fire in these three areas:
    A.

    B.

    C.

2. With the Lord's help, I WILL RE-IGNITE today!

Private Thoughts:

A Personal Devotion Just For You

Believe In You!

Trust, reliance upon, being persuaded about being confident in—all ways to describe the word belief. True belief. To believe in you, you must trust yourself, rely on yourself, have confidence in yourself and be persuaded about yourself. In a sentence, "you must know yourself in order to believe in yourself."

Knowing yourself will net you victories in your life. Believing in anyone starts with a relationship. Believing in yourself starts with a relationship with you. Knowing your hopes, your fears, processing your feelings, your emotions. Knowing your limitation, your goals, your strengths and yes, your weaknesses. Learning to trust your decisions. Learning how to make the best decisions for you.

Do you like you? Do you enjoy your own company? You must! Not in an arrogant, sheltered, closed off way, but in a loving, healthy, pampering way. The Bible says that we can only love others according to the love we have for ourselves.

Why is it important to believe in you? 'Cause when "they" talk about you, dog you out, lie on you, leave you, crucify you, you need to know that come "hell or high water" you can make it, you can get over it, they can talk but they can't change or alter who you are! You need to know you can make it!

Time is your friend when talking about believing in you. Begin to get to know you—then relax and trust yourself— rely on you…have confidence in you!

Believing in you—the foundation to a victorious life!

Use Affirmation #22 from 31 Days to a New You today. It says, " I lay aside, strip off, and throw off any weights, issues or people who try to stop me from running my race!"

Empowerment Action Plan:

1.   I trust these things about myself:
      A.

      B.

      C.

2.   I have confidence about myself in these areas:
      A.

      B.

3.   I need to believe in myself!

Private thoughts:

A Special Section For You...

CHAPTER TWELVE

A Bill Of Rights
For Today's Black Woman

*A Bill of Rights is a summary of fundamental rights and privileges guaranteed to a people.
The following is a Bill of Rights for YOU, today's Black woman.*

YOU HAVE THE RIGHT TO:
- Be FREE of stress, anxiety, guilt, frustration, aggravation and the ignorance of people who've not been where you've been or done what you've done.
- Hold your head high and to walk in your full stature of dignity, honor and respect.
- NOT to be anybody's doormat, maid, mama (if they're full grown), punching bag or sex slave.
- Better yourself, to dream big dreams, to have great visions, to hope for a better tomorrow and to accomplish ALL of your heart's desires.
- Take time for yourself, pamper yourself and love yourself.
- Be a wife, be a mother, be a sister, an aunt, a grandmother or a friend.
- Be big-breasted, big-hipped, thin, full-figured, short, tall, bald, permed, relaxed, weaved, dyed,

light, dark, mixed or whatever you've been blessed to be.
- ONE loving, caring, sharing, understanding and working brother.
- Be judged by your hard work, determination, ambition, attitude, strengths and abilities—and NOT by the color of your skin.
- Continue our heritage as strong, solid, stable and satisfied sisters.

May God's richest blessings be yours!

A Woman Of Excellence

*A Woman of Excellence is a female copy of God
that is of great value and superior quality*

She is **VALUABLE**: of great value or price!
She is **TRUSTWORTHY**: reliable!
She is **GRACIOUS**: kind, courteous, noble and charming!
She is **PLEASANTLY UNPREDICTABLE**: full of
surprises!
She is **ORGANIZED**: uniting the separate element of her
life into a smoothly working unit!
She is **SHREWD**: she's astute, quick-witted and keen in
discernment!
She is **HARD-WORKING**: she puts forth a constant effort!
She is **CONFIDENT**: trustworthy, sure, bold, self-assured
and optimistic!
She is **DILIGENT**: she constantly pays persistent attention
to her work!
She is **COMPASSIONATE**: she's moved to do something!
She is **PREPARED**: putting things in readiness!
She has **STYLE**: she's not concerned about the latest fad;
she's concerned about her overall quality of life!
She **BOOSTS OTHERS**: she shoves others upward;
she lifts them from below!
She is **GIFTED**: she's endowed with unique talents and
abilities!
She is **OPTIMISTIC**: she has the belief that good will
prevail!

She is **WISE**: having the power of discerning and judging rightly!

She is **SELF-CONTROLLED**: she exercises power over herself; she restrains herself!

She is a **MANAGER**: she is the one who directs any operation!

She is **RESPECTED**: she is treated with special consideration of high regard!

She is **REVERENT**: she is in <u>awe</u> of God and respects His authority!

The result of being this Woman of Excellence is that you will be blessed—empowered to prosper— all the days of your life!

PROVERBS 31 Virtuous Woman!

This list of "action statements" will encourage your heart. You'll discover that by God's design, the virtuous woman has a lot of action going on in her life...read, know that this is talking about Y-O-U...and be blessed!

Action statements of the Virtuous Woman

1.   She is **found**.
2.   She is **worthy.**
3.   She **does** her **husband good.**
4.   She **seeks** wool and flax.
5.   She **willingly works.**
6.   She **brings** food from afar.
7.   She **rises** while it is yet night.
8.   She **provides** food.
9.   She **considers** fields for purchase.
10. She **girds** herself with strength.
11. She **strengthens** her arms.
12. She **perceives** that her merchandise is good.
13. She **stretches** out her hand to the distaff.
14. She **extends** her hand to the poor.
15. She **reaches out** her hands to the needy.
16. She is **not afraid.**
17. She **makes** tapestry.
18. She **makes** linen garments and **sells** them.
19. She's **clothed** with **strength** and **honor.**
20. She **opens** her **mouth** with **wisdom.**
21. She **watches** over **the ways** of her household.
22. She's **not idle.**

23.   She's **praised** by her husband and family.

Personal Thoughts:

20 Secrets To Success In Life!

Success is defined by you, determined by you, and executed by YOU! No one, nothing, no circumstance, inconvenience, situation or person can alter, stop or impede your success.

Over the years, I've found twenty character traits that all winners have. All of these traits, at some point over the years, I've developed and perfected in my life. Through executing them, I've been blessed tremendously and have found great success.

They're self-explanatory. Browse the list and those areas that you are "not so good in" begin to develop and you'll have a solid foundation laid for many years of success.

20 Secrets To Success In Life

1. Trust, reliance and submission to the Lord!
2. Be proactive.
3. Have a victor mentality, not a _victim_ mentality.
4. Live by _choice_ not chance.
5. Build and maintain relationships.
6. Serve others.
7. Be unselfish.
8. Become a life-long learner.
9. Have a complete understanding and knowledge of yourself.
10. Be persistent.

11. Have a strong drive, determination and will to get it done.
12. Be a person of the highest integrity and morals.
13. Be honest.
14. Have an on going self-development plan.
15. Have pure motives in the things you do.
16. Get ready...hard work is required.
17. Have confidence.
18. Mentor others—GIVE BACK!
19. Be focused.
20. Have perseverance, never give up, cave in or quit.

GOD BLESS YOU ALWAYS!

Personal Thoughts:

Author Biography
JENNIFER KEITT (Kitt)
Founder/Host
Today's Black Woman Corporation

Powerhouse speaker and motivator Jennifer Keitt reaches more than 300,000 women weekly with one simple truth: "there is hope ... you can be victorious over life every day!" As founder of Today's Black Woman Corporation, Jennifer uses her frank yet compelling style to deliver a practical and timeless message to thousands across the nation who hear her speak.

Under TJ Communications Inc., the parent company she co-founded and heads with her husband Tony, Jennifer oversees the day-to-day operation of Today's Black Woman Corporation. Using Today's Black Woman Corporation as a platform, Jennifer produces the Today's Black Woman Radio Show with Jennifer Keitt; Today's Black Woman Online web site; and an interactive, motivational workbook. She also hosts conferences through Today's Black Woman Foundation including _the_ "Focus On You" Conference Series and the Joshua Generation Young Adult Outreach. Additionally, she frequently speaks at conferences and seminars across the country.

Jennifer's vision to "empower, educate, equip and encourage" is worked out daily in her personal roles as wife and mother of four children. Her vision as a professional was born in Chicago, several years after she graduated from college in Birmingham, Alabama. Before arriving in Chicago Jennifer spent six years perfecting her journalistic talents in roles such as reporter and producer at television stations in Birmingham; Quad Cities, Iowa; and Rochester, New York.

When she arrived in Chicago, Jennifer took her love for feature reporting and created a radio show to make a difference in the lives of Black women across the country. Jennifer and her husband launched TJ Communications Inc., and subsequently the Today's Black Woman Radio Show with Jennifer Keitt was born. The daily radio show is produced and distributed by TJ Communications, a multi-faceted company which also offers radio consulting, media production, event planning, print publishing and syndication.

Jennifer's voice communicates a deep sense of compassion in the radio show, web site, conferences and newsletters she produces yet she delivers all these with a renegade, "boot camp"-style approach. Her desire to win lives for Christ is evident in the excellent standard she commands of herself and others.

Jennifer lives with her husband and their four beautiful children.

For booking Jennifer Keitt for your next event or for more information on our company, contact us at:

Jennifer Keitt
Today's Black Woman Radio Show Inc.
Toll-Free
888-TB-WOMAN

www.todaysblackwomanradio.com
tbwoman@bellsouth.net

Visit us online today @ www.todaysblackwomanradio.com

GOD BLESS YOU ALWAYS!